Homeland Security And Economic Prosperity

Homeland Security And Economic Prosperity

Defending Our Country and the Survival of American Capitalism

Stephen J Feinberg

iUniverse, Inc.
New York Lincoln Shanghai

Homeland Security And Economic Prosperity
Defending Our Country and the Survival of American Capitalism

iUniverse, Inc.

For information address:
iUniverse, Inc.
2021 Pine Lake Road, Suite 100
Lincoln, NE 68512
www.iuniverse.com

ISBN: 0-595-27142-1

Printed in the United States of America

In memory of my parents whose love and generosity enabled me to become a student of game theory

Contents

INTRODUCTION

THE CRISES OF **2003**

The winter of 2002-2003 is a time of great crisis in America. Our physical safety is endangered by the threat of terrorist acts which might occur anywhere at any time. Our economic well being is threatened by a precipitous decline in the value of securities and our economy has stagnated and is in danger of collapse.

Thanksgiving is a time when we gather our families together to celebrate our good fortune in living in America. Our founding fathers gathered together to give thanks even though they were living in a hostile environment. As we gathered our families for Thanksgiving in 2002 we did so knowing that terrorists reside within our peaceful environment. Even the joyous feeling of Christmas was muted.

The attacks of September 11 exposed our domestic vulnerability to acts of terror. It is frightening to think how unprepared we were and still are. It is highly unlikely that we will be able to avoid further terrorist attacks unless we make a much more strenuous effort to improve our homeland defenses against future acts of terrorism.

While it is apparent that homeland security intelligence has been significantly upgraded since the events of September 11, we are told repeatedly that there is, nevertheless, a strong probability that further acts of terrorism are planned and will be carried out. We seek to answer two questions: "What is the best course of action our Government should take to deal with the threat of and win the war against domestic terrorism?" and "What is the best course of action our Government should take to return our economy to prosperity?"

The fear that gripped the nation after September 11 threatened to bring our economy to a halt. Our leaders rightfully encouraged us to get on with our lives lest these devastating acts of terrorism be permitted to succeed in destroying our way of life. Simply put, the premise was that we are a strong and resilient nation which should defy the terrorists and go on living our lives as before and rely on our federal and state governments to protect us from further acts of terrorism. Now, more than a year later, except for the area around Ground Zero, we have

1

returned to almost normal life, even in New York. Air traffic is down, but most of us are flying again and tourism shows signs of recovering, subject to the effects of the fear of terrorism and the worldwide recession. We know that no matter how many future terrorist acts may occur within our country, we must continue to conduct our lives in as normal a manner as possible to prevent terrorists from ever achieving their goal.

It is mystifying that despite the clear and present danger of a further terrorist attack within our country anywhere at any time, a great majority of Americans seem to have no sense as to how one fights a war against domestic terror. They know that the CIA and the FBI are seeking to round up terrorists around the world, and have heard of terrorist arrests abroad. Most Americans seem to be confused as to where the war is being fought as a result of the long time period that has elapsed since September 11 without a further attack, our military responses overseas and the discussion about our plans to replace the government in Iraq. Have we forgotten that terrorists living in our country attacked vital structures in New York and Washington on September 11?

We appear to be relying on hope and prayer that by some miracle the FBI will intercept all of the terrorists before any further acts are carried out and that we will be able to prevent other terrorists and weapons of mass destruction from entering our country. Where is our vision as to what must be done immediately to prevent or enable us to respond to further acts of terrorism within our country?

Villainous leaders of rogue countries who do not even respect the rights of their own people possess and are developing weapons of mass destruction and are a threat to their neighbors while claiming that they are the aggrieved parties. They can be expected to deliver any weapon that they have or develop to terrorists for use against us and our allies.

We know that if weapons of mass destruction are placed in the hands of fanatical terrorists, they can be expected to use them. Many of them are encouraged by their leaders to be prepared to die in the name of God as martyrs for their cause, to obtain promised rewards in their next life. There is a clear and present danger that they might kill or seriously injure thousands, tens of thousands, hundreds of thousands or even millions of people almost anywhere in America or anywhere in the world in a brief period of time. Terrorist groups exist in almost all countries. They pose a serious threat not only to our people and our way of life, but also to the survival of mankind.

President Bush has spearheaded the drive to improve homeland security. Democrats are putting up the customary united front in time of war. Under the President's leadership a bipartisan Congress passed legislation to create the

Homeland Security Department and to improve FBI intelligence gathering and support state and local actions to prevent future acts of terrorism. We are relying heavily on the enhanced efforts of the Immigration Service and Customs Service to seal our borders and the FBI's ability which has been improved by new investigative powers and a more determined effort to track down terrorists in our midst before they act.

Congress has made it clear that they will stand behind our President if he invades Iraq or takes other responsible military actions. They will also continue to support his homeland defense initiatives. Yet, both parties have let themselves be distracted by matters that, no matter how important, pale by comparison with dealing with the terrorist threat. They have returned to partisan politics and business as usual. We must resolve to make our country safe from acts of terror. The President appears to have devoted too much of his attention to matters overseas and not enough to dealing with the threat of domestic terrorism. He must refocus our efforts and take the lead in making the fight against domestic terror a bipartisan effort. If our politicians make America safe against acts of terror they will have ample time to carry out their party politics.

Our efforts are being constrained by cost concerns. We must be prepared to spend whatever is required to defend our nation to the best of our ability and make sacrifices as necessary. We must rearrange our priorities. Instead of focusing on what we cannot afford, we should recognize that homeland security is our number one priority and is required despite the enormity of the cost. We must not forget education, healthcare and other important domestic programs, but their importance is secondary to the need to protect our safety. How many parents who staunchly demand increased aid to education will be afraid to send their children to school if there is serious terrorist activity in their immediate neighborhood? We must be prepared to use less energy, do without some luxuries and make other sacrifices as may be necessary to defend our country.

As discussed below, a strong economy is important to support the war effort and to enable us to withstand future terrorist acts. The best way to ensure a strong economy is for our citizens to live in a manner as close to normal as practicable and for our government to increase spending on homeland security.

Despite the grave danger Americans seem more concerned with the stock market collapse and their personal financial woes. We are virtually clueless as to how our lives may be impacted by the war and have been given little advice as to what we should be doing individually and as a nation to prepare for future attacks and to defend ourselves. The majority of Americans have unquestioning faith in President Bush and are confident that he, and the formidable military he commands will protect us from further harm.

We remain extremely vulnerable to further attacks. We have ceremoniously honored those who performed heroically during the September 11 crisis and its aftermath and have displayed compassion and given financial support to the families of the victims. However, we lack a sense of urgency and have not taken adequate steps to protect our population from further attacks. Most of us do not know what we should do in the event of a terrorist attack using a chemical, biological or dirty nuclear weapon. Why are we not conducting civil defense drills around the country to prepare our citizens to deal with the after effects of terrorist acts? Hopefully many of the concerns expressed herein will never come to pass.

The President responded promptly and admirably to the events of September 11. However, in the more than a year which has passed since then we have failed to take adequate steps to defend our homeland. We must go much further in dealing with the homeland security emergency which existed then and will continue to exist throughout our lifetimes as well as those of our children and grandchildren. The President proposed the Homeland Security Department but he did not request adequate funding for such department to enable us to attain a state of readiness to fight a war against domestic terrorism. We should (i) enlarge the size of the FBI and other federal security agencies to enable them to track down terrorists in our midst and prevent future terrorist acts (ii) promptly seek subsidies for states and cities to subsidize police, national guards and civil defense teams and prepare them to prevent or deal with further acts of terror, (iii) seek sufficient increases in our military budget and enlarge our military to permit us to fight on multiple fronts, (iv) take adequate steps to securely seal our borders and (v) most importantly recognize the need for a federal identification card to enable us to identify and restrict the movement of terrorists within our country and create a task force to design and issue such a card and equipment needed to support it. We must be prepared to devote a much larger percentage of our GDP to defense and particularly to homeland security.

GAME THEORY

Game theory comes into play in numerous aspects of our lives, including all competitive sports, in running a business, making investment decisions or managing the family budget. Most people believe that America's most important games are baseball, football and basketball, though they might argue about which comes first, in order of popularity. However it is clear that our most important games, which affect the lives of all Americans, are the games of war, macroeconomics. and investing. To win at these games we must make moves that will enable us to defend our country and create prosperity.

The following chapters discuss how the games of war, macroeconomics and investing are played, examine recent events which have taken place in playing each of the games and the interrelationship of each of them to the others. They examine the reasons for the decline of our economy and the stock market indexes, the serious risk of deflation or a depression and the interrelationship between homeland security spending, a stock market recovery and a return of our economy to prosperity. They expose the risk that despite our unparalleled military might and generally strong economy we could, if we fail to make appropriate moves, wind up as losers in playing these games. The complexities of the issues and time constraints limit this writing to an attempt to examine the current status of each of the games and delineate strategies to be followed and moves to be made, some in more detail than others, in playing the games of war, macroeconomics and investing.

This writing will be frozen in time, but we will be able to look back and measure our progress and success in maintaining our unparalleled way of life.

THE GAME OF WAR

Historians know that war always has been, and always will be, the ultimate game of man. War is competitive but is not played for sport, enjoyment or entertainment. War is a game played, for among other reasons, to attain or maintain power and to seek vengeance. It has been played since civilization began. It is a game played with limited rules which seem to be enforced against only the weaker players, and there is no meaningful officiating. Generally the aggressor selects an enemy which it seeks to conquer or destroy and launches an attack at the enemy's most vulnerable areas. The attacking force has the element of surprise and can select the points of attack and the manner of attack at each point.

Defending against an attack is the most difficult aspect. To defend yourself you must be prepared to guard all areas of vulnerability except a territory which your are prepared to yield to the aggressor because it is indefensible or for some reason you determine it is unwise or unnecessary to defend. If you fear an attack you must consider making preemptive strikes to weaken the enemy to thwart or lessen the attack. If you elect not to make the first strike you should prepare to counterattack.

In the game of war one's military strength, both offensive and defensive, is of vital import, but the stronger side does not always win. Each game of war is different. Strategy, the unique circumstances of the battlefield and the element of surprise play an important role. The British learned this lesson during the U.S. Revolutionary War. When attacked a people has the option of surrendering and enduring the consequences, including living under the control of the conqueror. To some people this is not an acceptable alternative and they are prepared, as in the case of the Roman siege of Masada, to die rather than surrender.

Americans love to play all kinds of games and do so with unparalleled skills. We have proven our adeptness in the game of war whenever our freedom was at risk.

Weapons, the equipment of war, and the means of transporting and utilizing such weapons have changed and gotten more sophisticated and powerful over time. Weapons have evolved over the centuries from clubs, fire and stones to spears, arrows, swords and knives, canons, guns, bombs of ever increasing force and we know that other weapons of mass destruction are being developed. Methods of transporting men and weapons have evolved from walking and running to horseback, boat, truck, jeep, tank, plane and guided missile. As weapons and methods of delivery evolved and became more sophisticated, man devised the best available means of defense. We moved to high land and built walls and armed fortresses, formed nations and alliances and trained armies to defend them. We learned to use offensive weapons for defensive purposes and developed defensive weapons designed to counter the changing offensive threats. Warning systems evolved from shouts of alarm and smoke signals to sophisticated radar, spy planes and satellite surveillance. Along the way the nations that were incapable of defending themselves were destroyed and disappeared. However, as weapons became more powerful and sophisticated it became clear that no defenses were impregnable.

THE US PREPAREDNESS FOR WAR

The Nazi war to attempt to conquer and rule the world might have succeeded if the US, though generally unprepared for war and with its fleet crippled by Pearl Harbor, had not risen magnificently to the occasion. Our people volunteered or were drafted in unprecedented numbers to risk their lives to defend freedom and served heroically. Our civilians, men and woman, worked day and night, lived with rationing and joined together to give maximum support to our military. We rallied together to a common cause and succeeded. We had no interest in annexing the conquered lands. We occupied Europe for a short period and then withdrew. We craved peace, but before long we faced a new threat from Communist aggression and particularly from the USSR.

The United States during the last half of the 20th Century determined never to forget Pearl Harbor and cognizant of the threat of Communism, developed the greatest offensive force in the history of mankind, and sophisticated defensive weaponry to crush our enemies and defend ourselves and our allies against invasion by air, sea and land. Our efforts were financed by a burgeoning economy fostered by our free and open democratic society. Less prosperous nations were unable to match our accomplishments and their weapons became outmoded. We showed the world that we had the might to retaliate anywhere.

Although pockets of violence existed around the globe, we grew to believe we could protect ourselves, our allies and our vital interests from attacks from rogue countries. However, we learned from Viet Nam that our superior weaponry alone could not win a game of war against an enemy that hid in caves and was indistinguishable from the people we were defending. We withdrew from Viet Nam because it was sapping our spirit and because it became clear that defending South Viet Nam was not vital to our interests.

Our successful response to the Iraqi invasion of Kuwait was confirmation of our justifiable reliance on our military to protect us. After the war, we quickly withdrew our forces from Iraq, leaving its government intact, to further demonstrate that we seek peace and not to conquer our enemies and capture their land or seize the spoils of war. We demonstrated to the world that not only do we try to avoid the game of war, but also that when we are forced to play, we seek to minimize casualties on both sides and end the game as soon as possible. In the 1980s after the Soviet Union collapsed, the United States remained the only superpower. Most Americans felt more secure than at any time in our nation's history. We foolishly thought that no nation would ever again challenge us to a game of war. We talked of creating an impregnable "Star Wars" defense but failed to implement it. September 11 taught us that it would not have protected us against the new type of attack and weaponry.

THE WAR AGAINST TERRORISM

Our military superiority may be the principal reason that we paid scant attention as Al Qaeda trained an army of terrorists and attacked within our shores by bombing the World Trade Center in 1993. We caught the perpetrators and made a halfhearted effort to gather intelligence which might enable us to prevent a further attack. It was inexplicable that we did not treat that attack as an act of war. Why didn't we take steps to seal our borders at that time?

In the following years, we hardly paid attention when terrorists from time to time attacked our embassies around the world. We knew that Al Qaeda was recruiting and training an armed force. We knew that they were receiving financial support from so-called friendly nations whose policies permitted acts of terrorists to be praised and encouraged within their territory. We permitted such actions even though many such nations were ruled by dictatorships which relied on our military or economic support to maintain power.

Despite the heightened tensions in the Middle East we allowed a small boat filled with explosives to severely damage one of our important Naval vessels. The officers in charge aboard the USS Cole disgracefully permitted the attack without making any effort to defend the ship and the personnel on board. It is basic military strategy to protect your perimeter. We knew that Yemen had uncontrolled terrorist groups. The weapons and methods of delivery in the game of war were again changing rapidly and our leadership was slow to recognize it. It was clear that terrorists were reverting to easily constructed bombs as their weapons of choice and were using basic means of transportation. They took a chance that despite our sophisticated equipment, we would not intercept an unidentified small craft as it approached our ship.

Why didn't we intercept the attacking craft? No person, boat or vehicle should have been permitted to get within 100 yards of our ship. This was gross negligence either by the failure to give orders to defend against such acts or, if orders were given, in the performance by those responsible for carrying out the orders. Our TV networks competed for audiences by using advanced communications equipment to quickly generate programs showing pictures of the damage. The talking heads appeared to speculate as to who the attackers were. Why was there no outrage expressed by our leadership, the news media or our citizens over our failure to defend ourselves?

We lost a skirmish in the game of war because we failed to recognize, or chose to ignore, that it had begun. Could it be that we, like other superpowers throughout history, are incapable of adjusting to a new type of war which our enemy has crafted?

Our people trust our government to protect them. Our Presidents made a futile attempt to deal diplomatically with the rapidly growing threat of terrorism. We were attempting to cut off their funding and to restrict their operations, but we made little progress. Neither we nor the countries whose assistance we were seeking were talking directly to the terrorists. Apparently we were at a snail's pace developing a plan to deal with Al Qaeda, but there was no sense of urgency.

During the 1990s we foolishly tried to negotiate with Saddam Hussein over his wanton disregard of his inspection agreements which were a condition of the cease-fire in the Gulf War. Instead of giving him years to develop weapons of mass destruction and to amass billions of dollars to aid terrorism and expand his capacity to attack his neighbors, we should have given him an ultimatum relative to inspection on our terms and launched a defensive strike if he did not comply promptly. He made us look like cowardly fools in the eyes of the world. Although we continued to seek a diplomatic solution, our failure to respond militarily for such a long period of time made us look like bullies in the eyes of the world when we finally threatened to respond to Saddam's failure to comply with his agreements and UN resolutions.

We misjudged the threat of a terrorist attack on our homeland. We knew that terrorist cells existed around the world, but inexplicably never gave serious thought of guarding against the possibility that such cells might be developing in our own country. We knew that our intelligence and security agencies needed to be upgraded and were not well coordinated. We had ample warning and should have known that we were vulnerable to and in grave danger of an attack within our shores.

SEPTEMBER 11

While we were burying our heads in the sand, Osama bin Laden was engaged in planning his strategy for a game of war. Like military leaders throughout history he studied our defenses and weaknesses. He knew that he could not obtain or find a way to attack us with sophisticated weaponry. He planned a new way to attack by taking advantage of the vulnerability of our open society which had foolishly given up any meaningful attempt to prevent people from illegally entering or remaining in our country. Terrorists slipped into out country unnoticed among the wave of illegal immigrants and visitors pouring into the "melting pot." Osama bin Laden planted operatives in our midst who were inexplicably welcomed at our flight schools.

At the appointed hour, the terrorists attacked the very heart of capitalism, turning our majestic jets, one of our finest engineering accomplishments, into powerful weapons against us. They wantonly and deliberately killed thousands of innocent civilians. A new weapon of war had been created and used against us with devastating force. We soon realized how vulnerable we are. We learned that as a result of today's means of transportation, communication and weapons terrorists can change the form of war. We discovered that 19 terrorists had moved freely within our borders and had turned themselves into a new form of suicide bomber. Our radar and surveillance planes, military jets, submarines, aircraft carriers and guided missiles were useless against this kind of attack. We could only guess as to how many terrorists had entered our country and were preparing to carry out further terrorist acts of similar or even greater magnitude.

In recent years, terrorists have drastically changed the rules, the weapons and the methods of delivery in the game of war. We have learned that persons prepared to die for a cause, even children, can deliver on foot, powerful bombs which are easy to make. Explosives strapped to suicide bombers have become powerful weapons in the game of war. Commercial energy sources can be seized and converted into weapons. September 11 made it crystal clear that America is vulnerable to further terrorist attacks. We suddenly realized that terrorists in our midst could plant explosives almost anywhere at any time. It takes a much different type of effort to defend and protect your territory and property in this kind of war. September 11 focused our attention on the fact that other weapons of war, weapons of mass destruction, which we knew were being developed, were a clear and present threat to our survival at some unpredictable time in the future. Terrorists will select the weapons which they will use for each attack and the method of delivery. We must prevent them from successfully carrying out any further attacks within our homeland.

While the collapse of the Twin Towers may have been beyond Osama bin Laden's expectation, when we look back we can surmise that he sought to attain more than killing and injuring a large number of our people. He clearly planned to win the war by destroying our airline industry and crippling our economy and by causing our citizens to panic from the fear of further acts of terror. He is likely to have calculated that his success would attract large numbers of additional converts from the downtrodden in other countries with large numbers of Muslims, who, on his command, would participate in revolutions to permit him to take control of one mid-eastern country after another. Although no such revolutions have yet taken place, he and Al Qaeda are revered in the slums of the Arab world.

THE US RESPONSE TO SEPTEMBER 11

September 11 was the wake-up call. Americans sat stunned as they watched the horrible events unfold on TV and were shocked to learn in the next few days how brazenly the terrorists had trained in the US and how easily they had passed through airport security.

President Bush responded immediately and decisively. He recognized and pronounced that the September 11 attack was an act of war. The game of war officially began. He made an historic decision when he identified the enemy as a group of terrorists and not the act of the country in which they resided and had taken control of. We suddenly realized that terrorist groups around the world, of which Al Qaeda is the most notorious, had been playing the game of war against us unopposed for almost ten years.

Our President immediately recognized the need for improving homeland security and for a prompt military response overseas. We were proud and pleased when he took charge, spearheaded the assault against the Taliban and Al Qaeda, appointed a homeland security officer to coordinate our security efforts and moved to change our laws to enable us to upgrade our intelligence gathering.

President Bush reaffirmed the principle that anyone giving support to terrorists is himself a terrorist. He boldly defined and criticized the "axis of evil" as supporters of terror. He could have listed fifteen or twenty other countries. Soon thereafter he invoked discussion about invading Iraq to prevent further development of weapons of mass destruction. He recognized the importance of taking preemptive actions against terrorists wherever they might be found. A large majority of the American people trusted him and approved of his initial actions. Our efforts in Afghanistan and elsewhere around the world have disrupted Al Qaeda activities, but we were not well prepared and the effort was flawed. Many of the terrorists escaped and regrouped in Pakistan and Iran or have regrouped in other countries. We have learned again that it is difficult to retaliate if you can't find the enemy and are concerned about injuring civilians. Furthermore, the ability to retaliate against or track down terrorists overseas doesn't prevent attacks at home from persons who are already here.

Groups of terrorists living throughout the world, some of which are receiving financing and weapons from rogue countries, are affiliated with and supporting other terrorists and developing plans to attack us and our allies. Dealing militarily and politically with the problem of the incubation and arming of terrorists, including preventing the development of weapons of mass destruction, is of vital importance to defending our homeland.

As a country that has respected all religions since its inception, we have a difficult time dealing with the fact that a significant number of Muslims interpret their religion as demanding the jihad which is being waged against the US and all non-Muslims. We must find a way to isolate and track down those Muslims and any other groups who plan to attack us and those who give them support. The task is complicated because the enemy will hide among groups of peaceful Muslims.

Unfortunately our actions are constrained by our desire to avoid civilian casualties if possible, our and our allies' needs for oil, our need to obtain the cooperation of our allies and unreliable local governments in our hunt for terrorists and our attempts at political correctness. Obviously we do not wish to fight the war against terrorism alone. Nevertheless, it is difficult to comprehend why we continue to supply arms and financial aid to countries that encourage the teaching of hatred against us.

We must concurrently enhance our efforts to provide protection and assistance to law abiding Muslims who reside around the world. We must find a way to ensure that our humanitarian aid reaches them and does not wind up in a Swiss bank account of a corrupt leader. We might consider proposing UN protected enterprise zones within impoverished countries to provide jobs, food and housing.

It is not the purpose of this writing to discuss a political solution or the advisability of taking military actions outside the US even though such actions may be important to protect our safety and the safety of our allies. Instead it deals with the actions we should take domestically to protect our citizens and our property. We should note that: (i) the effectiveness of the execution of our counterattack against terrorism appears inconsistent, beginning with the invasion of Afghanistan, (ii) until recently our efforts were inadequately justified and explained to Americans, our allies or to our enemies (iii) we must be prepared to take substantial risks to deter or delay the development of weapons of mass destruction, (iv) we must modify our relationship with countries with large Muslim populations whose actions are constrained by the risk of a terrorist led revolt, (v) certain of our allies have in the previous century proven themselves incapable of recognizing the danger of impending war and of defending themselves, (vi) it is impossible to predict with any degree of certainty, the positive or adverse consequences of any military action we are considering and (vii) although we generally try to avoid civilian casualties, less that 60 years ago, one of our great presidents authorized dropping atom bombs on our enemy in time of war to reduce future loss of American lives. Our President appears to be receiving excellent advice on these matters. He must carefully weigh all his options.

DEFENDING AGAINST DOMESTIC TERRORISM

It is the terrorists within our midst who present the gravest immediate danger. Our unprecedented financial success, which peaked in the 90s, enabled us to establish an unparalleled infrastructure which has left us vulnerable to terrorist attack. Although more than a year has passed since September 11, Al Qaeda has historically carefully planned its attacks. We have every reason to believe and are constantly reminded that other terrorists remain in our country and that another terrorist act of great magnitude may occur at almost any time.

The Israelis have learned that despite a highly trained and competent security force and a population alert to signs of danger, the prevention of terrorist acts carried out by individuals, even children, prepared to die, is almost impossible. The Israeli war against terrorists has demonstrated that even if you send in tanks and soldiers to track down the terrorists, it is difficult to do so. This is particularly true when they blend in with and have the sympathy of the local community, encouraged by religious leaders. We only have to observe the horrifying deaths and injuries inflicted by suicide bombers on Israel to know that we must prevent such types of attacks here.

Americans face a graver risk of random death from war than at any other time in our history. When hydrogen bombs threatened our survival in the 1960s, we knew that the USSR was concerned that our Government had the capacity to retaliate and that victory was impossible for them. There was very little ordinary citizens could do to prepare ourselves for a nuclear attack by plane or missile.

The dangers of terrorism are still in their infancy. Al Queda and similar groups of religious cults have been training and arming their followers as terrorists for more than ten years during which we have maintained virtually open borders, which has enabled them to infiltrate operatives within our society. As a result, we do not know how many terrorists are living within our country. We will be extremely fortunate if it is only a small number. We know that there are tens of thousands of terrorists and millions of disgruntled Muslims throughout the world who openly display hatred towards us.

Some of them claim and use as an excuse, that their hatred is based on our support of Israel. That is not the only reason. They view the US as a Christian country and feel disgraced and humiliated when they compare our power and prosperity with the widespread helplessness and poverty in most Muslim controlled countries. They view our efforts to promote female equality as a threat to their male dominated society. It is small wonder that they are easily convinced by their leaders that God commands and will reward acts of terror against us. They are led to believe that Muslims should be proud of and rejoice in acts of terror that they carry out. Their hatred will be fueled as it is in Israel by our killing of terrorists around the world in our self defense, but with unavoidable civilian casualties which will be multiplied because our enemies will hide among innocent men, woman and children. Others will seek revenge for loss of a terrorist relative.

Despite our efforts to gather intelligence after September 11, it seems clear from numerous government pronouncements that we do not know what other tactics Osama bin Laden, or if he is dead, his accomplices and successors, may have in store to try to punish and destroy us to enable them to win the game. It has been alleged that certain of our citizens helped to fund Al Qaeda. We do not know how many American citizens or residents are acting with or supporting terrorists or how many are susceptible of being recruited in the future.

We know that because the nineteen September 11 terrorists were all Muslims born in middle eastern countries, many American Muslims have been carefully scrutinized by the FBI in its attempt to locate terrorists. We must remain diligent in protecting the Constitutional rights of our Muslim citizens and visitors who are not terrorists, but we must also make it crystal clear that we will arrest and try for treason any of our citizens who aid and abet terrorism or who might do so in the future.

We must develop the best strategies to enable us to defend ourselves and prevent Al Qaeda or other terrorists from winning the war no matter what means of attack they may have planned. We must start by asking ourselves the question: "How could we have anticipated and prevented the events of September 11?" Even if one argues that we could not have prevented September 11 from taking place, that merely emphasizes the importance of implementing a carefully conceived and painstakingly carried out effort to prevent any and all future terrorist acts. Regardless of fault by any of our leaders or security personnel for not anticipating September 11, we must diligently pursue terrorists in our midst wherever they may be and do our utmost to attempt to prevent or minimize the effect of further terrorist acts. That's what we must do to win the game of war which they have commenced.

President Bush has promised to do everything possible to prevent further acts of domestic terrorism. We should not overlook the significant steps he has instituted relative to intelligence gathering which have led to the identification and detention of some but obviously not all the terrorists residing within the US. Although we must recognize the need for secrecy in this area which has limited public disclosure as to the extent of the progress being made, it is clear that the effort must be further expanded.

Considering the gravity of the danger, we have barely made a meaningful start in this direction. This is the greatest emergency that our nation has ever faced. World Wars I and II placed our survival as a nation in jeopardy, but, except for Pearl Harbor, the enemy did not reach our shores during the past century. It dwarfs the Cuban missile crisis where we had a sane government with a fear of retaliation to deal with.

The most important aspect of the war against terror is preventing attacks within our homeland. Victories against terrorists overseas may be extremely important in weakening and disrupting the planned actions of the enemy but do not assure protection at home. Are we prepared to add terrorism to accidents and diseases as a leading cause of death in America? We have to decide if we are going to make an all-out effort as expeditiously as possible to defend our homeland or to make only a reasonable effort, relying on a small number of people and tightly controlled expenditures to deal with a difficult problem and take our chances that it will succeed, or that we will be able to upgrade the effort at a later time if needed.

THE ENORMITY OF THE TASK

We have hundreds of thousands of strategic places to protect, including all places where groups of people congregate, our borders, ports, landmarks, buildings, communication, transportation and power generation and transmission hubs and networks, our air, food and water supplies, oil refineries and storage facilities, oil and gas and hazardous material delivery networks, places where weapon making materials of any kind are sold and defense factories and facilities ("Strategic Places"). Our enemy may treat any of our Strategic Places as potential targets to attack next in the game of war.

Almost immediately after September 11, our leadership focused its efforts on calming our population, protecting airplane cockpits, upgrading airport security, the Ground Zero cleanup and on comforting and giving charity toward the victims' families. All of these acts were important and demonstrated that we are a strong, determined and caring people. This made great press for politicians and reporters and made us feel better.

While these were all commendable actions, they did very little to prevent other acts of terror. Even our attempts to improve airport and airplane security, a glaring weakness exposed by the acts of September 11 have been carried out in a suspect manner. We have taken steps to prevent use of our of planes as weapons of terror by strengthening cockpit doors and adopting a policy of shooting down planes which may be piloted by terrorists, if necessary to protect Strategic Places. Our own horrific act, though justifiable, would cost the lives of the innocent civilians aboard.

Though we may have greatly reduced the risk that our large planes will be used as missiles, airline security is still lax and it is highly doubtful that air travel is or will be safe from future terrorist attacks even after the new luggage screening procedures are in place. We have not taken adequate steps to attempt to protect our aircraft from acts of sabotage. The prospect of the existence within our country of portable rocket launchers, which can deliver heat-seeking missiles, requires us to develop as soon as practicable a means of preventing their use against our civilian aircraft.

It was relatively easy for Al Qaeda to turn our jets into weapons. We must anticipate and prevent terrorists from transforming any of our other energy sources into weapons. Our powerful military is prepared to protect us from attacks by air and sea, but its role does not include protecting our Strategic Places from a ground attack originating within the US. Where are our forces protecting our streets and our Strategic Places? Our Government seems to be issuing useless warnings so that if and when the next attack occurs our leadership will be able to say we were warned in advance.

It seems that Americans are either fatalistically accepting the risk, believing that our government will do the best it can to protect us or thinking they will not be directly affected. The recent sniper attack in the Washington D.C. area demonstrated how unprepared we are to capture or even prevent the movement of terrorists. Prior to September 11 we relied on the local police forces and the FBI to provide homeland security. The FBI was making a half-hearted attempt to track potential terrorists but was more accustomed to capturing terrorists after they commit acts of terror. After September 11 the main responsibility was given to the FBI which is now attempting to focus its efforts on prevention of terrorism but has insufficient manpower and funding to enable it to deal with the task. If we continue to permit terrorists to move freely within our country it is only a matter of time until they again turn one of our energy sources or use other types of weapons, including weapons of mass destruction, against us.

We have talked of improving the training of local police to be better able to deal with terrorism, but our financially weakened states are incapable of financing the effort without substantial Federal assistance. The recently formed Homeland Security Department is barely off the ground and is likely to be involved in political maneuvering for many months. How many terrorist acts have to occur before our leaders, who are responsible for our safety, take adequate steps and authorize sufficient funding to defend us against terrorism?

Except for low-key requests for Americans to be diligent and to report suspicious activity and talk of rewards of up to $25,000,000 (without describing the conditions which must be met to earn the reward,) we have been led to believe that there is not very much that an ordinary person can do to help protect our homeland from future acts of terrorism. What a terrible mistake. Terrorists prefer more primitive times and they are probably satisfied if they can cause great damage and inflict pain upon us, even if they cannot conquer us.

Our citizens can be of great help in preventing acts of terrorism of the type we must anticipate. As was the case in fighting World War II, we must get all Americans involved in the effort to protect our homeland. We must use television to elicit support and give guidance as to how all of us can help. The President must redirect our thoughts to the overriding importance of the war and particularly against domestic terrorism as our first priority. He must set forth a comprehensive plan to carry out an effort which must be of unprecedented magnitude.

We know from history that when Americans play the game of war, they play to win. Why are we not making a greater effort to win this war? If asked, the clear choice of the great majority of the American people would be that we, without further delay, undertake a maximum effort to seek the best defense available against terrorism. We must all be prepared to voluntarily limit some of our personal freedoms and comfort and be prepared to serve our country and to sacrifice financially if necessary, to contribute to our nation's defensive effort.

If given clear instruction as to how they can assist in defending our homeland, Americans will immediately respond. The question to be asked is whether our Government is carefully considering what our population can do other than to provide information to the FBI, if they happen to think about it. If our Government fails to take the lead in getting our citizens involved in homeland security we should be imploring our president and our congressmen to give us the opportunity to participate in the effort to protect our country.

A THREE-PRONGED EFFORT

Dealing with terrorism within our borders requires a three-pronged effort. First, we must identify and detain substantially all of the terrorists so that we can avoid or at least minimize the number of terrorist attacks. This will require the issuance of a national identification card discussed below.

Second, we must carry out an unprecedented effort to protect our homeland from further attacks which they brazenly advise us are planned. It is unlikely that we will be successful unless we restrict the freedom of movement of terrorists and at the same time take a broad array of actions to protect our Strategic Places. We must seal our borders and work with Canada and Mexico to prevent the entry of terrorists and weapons of mass destruction into our country.

Third, we must prepare to deal with the horrific consequences of our failing in our effort to prevent further terrorist acts.

Valuable time has been lost. We have not put forth our best effort to prevent a shadowy, hateful and elusive enemy from attempting to murder our people in as painful a manner as they possibly can and to destroy us emotionally and economically. Our peace and prosperity and our way of life are in jeopardy. We are not committing sufficient manpower or funding to deal with it appropriately. Until recently too much attention has been given to our country's plans to "kick butt" in Iraq, if necessary, and not enough to homeland security.

If we are going to win this game of war, we must demonstrate better defensive strategy and work together as a united nation in an all-out effort to prevent the movement of terrorists and their weapons within our country. In time of war our President must not act as a politician, but as the Commander-in-Chief. We cannot afford to wait for the next terrorist attack or the attacks after that. OUR PRESIDENT MUST ASSUME COMMAND OF OUR HOMELAND DEFENSE AND MOVE US FULL SPEED AHEAD TO WIN THE GAME OF WAR AGAINST DOMESTIC TERROR. WE MUST NOT FAIL!

IDENTIFYING, DETAINING AND LIMITING THE FREEDOM OF MOVEMENT OF TERRORISTS

The search to identify and detain potential terrorists before they carry out further acts of terrorism must become the number one priority in America. One of the lessons of September 11 is that a small number of terrorists can cause a major catastrophe. We now know that despite the fact that many of the 19 terrorists were on the FBI radar screens, they moved freely around the US. They all passed through airport security using their own names and were permitted to board planes on September 11. Prior to that they attended flight schools which attracted attention. We know now that we had sufficient intelligence for the events of September 11 to have been avoided if a routine security check at the airport had revealed the security risks of certain of the terrorists. The terrorists should have been identified and intercepted before they boarded the planes. We cannot turn back the clock and avoid those mistakes, but we can use our best efforts to avoid similar mistakes in the future.

Although the September 11 terrorists brazenly used their own names, we must expect that future terrorists will use aliases and obtain fake IDs to hide their identity. We must also expect that terrorists will use ways to attack without sacrificing their lives thereby creating the likelihood of a terrorist carrying out multiple attacks.

Because we are such an open society which failed to enforce our immigration laws for such an extended period of time and because of the enormity of our trade volume, we did virtually nothing to prevent the infiltration of terrorists and any weapons which may have been available to them including weapons of mass destruction. It is apparent that we have no reliable information as to the number of terrorists hiding in our country or as to nature of the weapons in their possession or what their plan of attack might be. We have been told there are hundreds of terrorist cells in our country, but except for one in Buffalo, NY we haven't identified any of them.

We should have learned from the events of September 11 and other terrorist acts around the world that the current risk of future terrorist acts must not be tolerated. We cannot permit terrorists to ride cars and trucks on our highways or walk our streets. Yet we are not making a serious attempt to prevent them from doing so. At the current time there is little or no coordination of the security information gathered by state and local police and the FBI and other national security agencies. It often takes months to solve serial crimes and we later discover that there was information in a local police record which if, known by others, could have led to the earlier capture of the perpetrators. We know that the current effort of the local police and the FBI is unlikely to prevent future terrorist acts or quickly capture the terrorists. We know that men tend to become bored or lazy and have limited memory capacity. We must find a way to coordinate the effort and use computers to enhance it. THIS GAME OF WAR IS DIFFERENT THAN ANY WE HAVE PLAYED BEFORE AND REQUIRES A NEW TYPE OF DEFENSE. The President's call for a national data-base is an important step in this direction.

We can not make a meaningful attempt to assure the safety of our streets and Strategic Places, unless we are prepared to limit freedom of movement of virtually everyone in our country. The importance of restricting the movement of terrorists was made crystal clear in the October 2002 sniper attacks in the Washington D.C. area. The terrorists there involved were limiting their attacks to individuals. Yet parents feared sending their children to school or letting them go to playgrounds and were themselves afraid to go to shopping malls and gas stations. We know that if mass murders are committed the concern will be of a much greater magnitude.

We read every day about another vulnerable location that terrorists may attack by air, land or sea, with disastrous consequences. We have to protect all of of our Strategic Places to the best of our ability. Certain Strategic Places, where a devastating effect may result from the explosion of even a small bomb, have to be given our greatest attention. Security checkpoints will have to be created or expanded at various points in our transportation network, including all bridges and tunnels and portable checkpoints created for use at roadblocks or on inner city roadways and sidewalks. It will be difficult but we will have to learn to adjust our lives to accept the presence of policemen and FBI agents or homeland security forces restricting our movement. Our leadership is procrastinating because they know that proposing limitations on our freedom of movement will not be well received. We must be prepared to live with the inconvenience.

Moreover, we must find a reliable way to ensure that we can quickly and correctly identify all of the people all of the time and accurately and instantly check all security and intelligence information available. We must do so in a way that minimizes business disruptions and interference with our daily lives and personal freedoms.

To restrict the freedom of movement of terrorists, we must, as soon as practicable, transform our country from one in which our people have almost unlimited privacy and freedom of movement into a society where we can track everyone's movement when they travel on our roads, walk our sidewalks and approach or enter Strategic Places. Although it will obviously be upsetting to all Americans to think that we will be inhibiting our right to move freely and that our Government will be tracking our every movement, the risk that millions of us may die at the hands of terrorists makes it necessary that we do so.

Many civil rights advocates will argue that restricting our freedom of movement is a violation of one or more of our Constitutional rights. They will argue that we must not permit "Big Brother" to control our lives. Based upon our prior experience with certain abusive law enforcement practices, there is good cause for concern. However, the most important role of our Government is to protect our person and our property. Those who would reject the creation of an identification system virtually guaranty that many of our citizens will needlessly die. What greater loss of Constitutional freedoms is there than the loss of one's life? In order to live safely we are going to have to voluntarily limit our freedom of movement. We learned in the 60's that we can live with curfews to keep rioters off the streets. We must learn to live with a security network to keep terrorists off our streets. We will have to be extremely diligent to prevent the identification system from being used as a basis to unfairly deny Constitutional protections to any person or group. The vigilance of our civil rights organizations can be expected to ensure that such protections will be honored.

IT IS IMPERATIVE THAT EVERYONE BE REQUIRED TO HAVE A SECURE NATIONAL PHOTO IDENTIFICATION CARD (A "US ID") WHICH, WHEN PRESENTED AT CHECKPOINTS TO BE ESTABLISHED, WILL WITH THE ASSISTANCE OF COMPUTERIZED EQUIPMENT RELIABLY CONFIRM THE CARD HOLDER'S IDENTITY TO ENABLE US TO ISOLATE, IDENTIFY AND TRACK POTENTIAL TERRORISTS. IT MUST BE THE CORNERSTONE OF THE PROJECT TO

RESTRICT THE MOVEMENT OF TERRORISTS AND ELIMINATE THEM FROM OUR COUNTRY.

The sole use of the US ID card should be to isolate, identify and restrict the freedom of movement of and lead to the detention, arrest or expulsion of terrorists. We might in the discretion of the FBI also use it to track felons or to assist in the taking of a census. None of the information collected should ever become available to the public or subject to subpoena for use in civil litigation. When applying for a US ID, or on a routine security check if they fail to apply for a US ID, terrorists will risk being exposed and apprehended. Without a US ID the task of identifying and meaningfully restricting the movement of substantially all of the potential terrorists is virtually impossible.

We must, concurrently with the issuance of the US ID cards, establish a Homeland Security Network ("HSN") under the control of the Homeland Security Department or the FBI to coordinate the efforts of the FBI and local police officers among others, to verify the identity of US ID cardholders and check their security status. Fixed and mobile identification checkpoints will have to be established throughout the country beginning as soon as we can. When the US ID cards are presented at a checkpoint, we will be able to instantly and accurately identify and check the security status of the cardholder. A reliable and secure state of the art communication network will have to be created as a part of the HSN, so that the FBI, other intelligence agencies and the local police can securely communicate with each other.

The pressing need for a US ID card may not be apparent to most Americans today. The need will become obvious if one or two domestic terrorist attacks take place. There are too many hotbeds of terror around the world and too many terrorists with large groups of followers who have billions of dollars available to them to develop weapons of mass destruction, to ignore the risk that an identification card will be needed tomorrow, next week, next year, five years from now or at any time in the foreseeable future. If we proceed diligently with the development and dissemination of US IDs and confirmatory equipment, we may succeed in having a reliable security system in place before weapons of mass destruction reach the hands of terrorists.

The effort to issue US ID cards should be carried out expeditiously. Moreover, we must, without further delay, while we issue US ID cards and develop and deploy required readers and scanners, take immediate action to protect our Strategic Places to the best of our ability. We can begin by establishing fixed and mobile checkpoints at which we can check currently available, though unreliable, identification such as driver's licences and credit cards. We must also where appropriate, subject to Constitutional safeguards, search vehicles and people for weapons and bombs at such checkpoints. As soon as practicable, we will have to develop the capacity to input into FBI computers all the information gathered with respect to the movement of all people throughout the country who pass through a checkpoint, so that it can be linked with all available security information.

THE US ID CARD

All residents and all persons entering our country should be required to apply for a US ID, which should ideally be issued upon presentation of a passport or birth certificate and completion of a basic information sheet. As a practical matter we have to accept other types of identification such as any photo ID, a driver's license or even a pay stub. Obviously the less reliable the identification document presented when applying for a US ID the more likely it is that people will be able to obtain a US ID using an alias. While the use of an alias when applying for a US ID should be made a criminal act, it will not materially impact the reliability of the system.

The identification information gathered at the time of the filing of the US ID application will be the basis for reliable identification of the card holder at all times after its issuance. Most aliases will be revealed over time as available security information is inputted into the HSN and cross checked against information supplied in US ID application forms and gathered at checkpoints.

The information sheet should request the applicant to supply information such as the applicant's (i) name, and other names used in the last ten years, (ii) address and prior addresses for the past three years, (iii) country of birth (iv)countries of citizenship and residence, (v) social security number (vi) personal characteristics, such as sex, hair color, weight and height and (vii) if not born in the U.S., the date and basis for entry into the U.S. All applicants should be digitally photographed and fingerprinted when filing an application and subjected to a retinal and facial scan to the extent practicable. The collection of a DNA sample should probably be delayed for a later time.

Because we will be using fingerprint or retinal scan matches for identification we can limit the information appearing on the face of the US ID card. It probably should contain your name and photograph and your assigned personal bar code. It should also contain the name of the country or countries of which you are a citizen or have been issued a passport. It need not contain your address or social security number, if you have one, or other applicable identification information. All of the information collected with the application as well as your bar code should be transferred to the FBI database and become a part of the HSN .

The responsibility for overseeing the issuance of the US IDs should probably be given to the FBI, but we could give it to the Homeland Security Department, the U.S. Postal Service, the Passport Office or a new office created for this purpose. It is pure folly, even laughable, to think as some have suggested, that state driver's licenses, can be used for accurate identification. State standards differ and driver's licenses are much too easy to counterfeit. Regulating drivers relates to qualification to operate a vehicle and does not warrant the same degree of security.

RAPID AND RELIABLE IDENTITY VERIFICATION

The issuance of an identification card alone is not sufficient to prevent the movement of and to track terrorists. To maximize the security benefits and prevent counterfeiting and misuse of the US ID card we must provide instantaneous fingerprint, retinal scanning and facial recognition equipment as they become available at checkpoints across the country, including every Strategic Place, police car and emergency vehicle, to permit rapid and reliable identity verification. US ID cards should be inspected prior to entering our Strategic Places and when boarding or when tickets are collected on all planes, trains and buses. There must be a randomness to the location of some of the checkpoints so that terrorists will not be able to devise ways to avoid them.

We must verify the identification of the holder of the card by transmitting the bar code and other information gathered at the checkpoint electronically over a secure communications network and checking them against the identifying characteristics gathered at the time one applies for a US ID and securely maintained in the FBI computer system. For identification purposes a person's assigned bar code will be more important than his name, and his fingerprints or retinal characteristics more important than his photograph. We must make it clear to people manning checkpoints that photo IDs are of limited value unless they are checked against the identifying characteristics and that no identification is complete until they have done so. To the extent practicable we must automate every step of the process.

The responsibility for providing the required readers and scanners and the communications network and supervising their use can be given to the agency issuing the US IDs or can be given to the FBI or the Homeland Security Department. We must determine what type of verification equipment is best suited for use at each checkpoint.

We should set a goal and an aggressive time frame for everyone who visits any of our Strategic Places or who rides on our highways or walks our streets to have a US ID card. We must with the secrecy and expediency of the Manhattan Project undertake an effort to develop the procedures and equipment to enable us to issue a secure US ID card and upgrade existing and develop new security devices. This immense task should have commenced on September 12, 2001.

Congress must immediately increase the size and funding of the agency selected to issue the US ID and to develop the necessary equipment.

We must not be dissuaded by the difficulty or cost of the task. We must not forget that the aggregate monetary damage caused by the events of September 11 exceeded a trillion dollars. With determination and effort we can accomplish what seems impossible. We got men to the moon and they returned alive. This task is infinitely more important. Our President should take charge and do it now.

LINKING OF SECURITY INFORMATION

A second function of the US ID will be to link all security information gathered by the FBI, CIA, other intelligence agencies and the local police, with the identification information. Hopefully the reports are true that since September 11 our various Federal intelligence agencies have greatly improved their sharing of information. Although the Homeland Security Department could be given the responsibility for securely maintaining the HSN database, the FBI which has an organization in place is better equipped to do so. We know from experience that unless it is in control of the database the FBI will be reluctant to share its information. We will have to be extremely careful that all security information wherever gathered by any security agency is accurately and instantly inputted into the HSN. We will have to develop software to instantly analyze all information available at any time.

Arrangements will have to be made to automatically and electronically transfer information from state and local data bases to the FBI computers. We will be able to continually gather information about US ID cardholders. For example, your address will be updated every time you apply for a drivers license, car registration or register to vote.

In order to expedite the issuance of the US ID cards, the initial security checks of an applicant for a US ID should be limited to searching existing CIA, FBI and other governmental security files to identify persons who are being sought as security risks. This will enable persons who are potential terrorists to obtain a US ID. Therefore, we must recognize that initially, US IDs will be of limited use for security purposes.

The issuance of the US ID cards will, however, immediately, from the time of issuance, provide an accurate means of identifying and tracking the cardholder. This will enable us to expand the use of the US ID over time, to enable it to be used as a principal element of a reliable security system. The issuance of US IDs will also be of immediate value in reducing the risk of acts by terrorists who may be in hiding, since if we establish checkpoints across the US, their movement will be constrained if they fail to obtain a US ID. Once they apply for a US ID they will be trackable by the HSN.

Each time your US ID is presented at any checkpoint that fact will automatically be inputted and stored in the FBI computer system. Whenever a vehicle is stopped at a checkpoint, car registration information and the presence in the vehicle of the driver and the passengers will be recorded. It will be available to match with all other information for tracking terrorists and felons. We will have to devise a system for quickly scanning the US ID cards and checking the identifying characteristics of every passenger in a vehicle.

Clearly discretion must be left with the FBI to determine when a person is identified at a checkpoint whether or not the individual is a holder of a US ID, if such person represents a security risk and should be restricted from entering any of our Strategic Places. The benefit of issuing US IDs will be greatly diminished if it enables even one terrorist, who should be excluded based on available security information, to gain access to a Strategic Place. We should recognize that it is highly probable that certain terrorists have been residing within our country for years and leading apparently exemplary lives. We will not be able to identify them or watch them closely until they or someone they are known to associate with commit an act detected by or brought to the attention of the FBI and imputed into the security network.

When a US ID is presented at any security checkpoint the computerized system will review all available identity and security information relating to such cardholder. Concurrently with his identity being confirmed, the FBI will determine whether a security issue exists with respect to such cardholder and be able to immediately give instructions to the persons manning the checkpoint and the local police (if they so desire) by visual and audio transmission. The FBI will also determine whether the person should be detained. To shorten the response time, the FBI will have to program responses into the system which deal with common situations such as criteria for denial of admission to a Strategic Place. With the help of the HSN, we may be able to thwart a terrorist plot in its infancy or to track a person who commits an act of terror or a felony.

President Bush must work with the Republican and Democratic leadership in advance to attempt to get support in Congress for the issuance of the US ID and the establishment of the HSN. He must justify the need for and describe the benefits of a US ID card to the American people.

This must be a bipartisan effort. We cannot afford to delay any longer the issuance to everyone of US ID cards while our Congress and Federal officials haggle with each other over the need, cost, propriety and content of such cards. We must issue US ID cards as soon as practicable linked to fingerprint and other backup information as current technology permits.

To induce applications for US IDs all work, visitor and student visas should be suspended if the holder fails, within a designated time frame, to file an application for a US ID.

Issuance of US ID cards will present immediate problems. Many of our citizens will object to any restriction on their freedom of movement. Some will refuse to apply or believe they do not have need for a US ID because of the location of their residence or for other reasons and may disregard the law and fail to apply for a US ID. Most of them will not be terrorists. This will not create a serious problem for them or the FBI until they decide to visit one of our Strategic Places or are stopped at a checkpoint. If they do so, their available identification information should be checked and inputted into the HSN together with their identifying characteristics. They should also receive a summons which should be easily vacated upon filing for a US ID.

Since the US ID will be issued without charge, very substantial Federal funding will be required. To enable the states and local governments to upgrade their police forces and to utilize their National Guards to provide maximum assistance to the HSN, Congress will have to subsidize a large portion of the costs. The issues with respect to the effect on our economy of the issuance and use of US IDs is discussed below in the section dealing with the US economy. We will have to determine what amount, if any, the Government will charge for making the security equipment available and for providing security information at checkpoints, in privately owned buildings, theaters, stadiums and elsewhere.

PRESERVING FREEDOM BY RESTRICTING FREEDOM OF MOVEMENT

We must never lose sight of the goal which is to ensure that our freedoms including the ability to raise our families in a safe environment and having the opportunity to pursue our dreams without fear of our safety are preserved. Our aim should be to get the US ID cards issued while avoiding confrontation with our citizenry to the extent practicable. However, we must not restrict our attempts to locate terrorists who remain in hiding while they are developing, awaiting delivery of or storing weapons of mass destruction. Once most Americans have been issued a US ID, persons arriving at a checkpoint without one will attract immediate attention.

The FBI will have to determine whether to permit certain movement, but to restrict other movement. For example, a foreign student issued a US ID would have freedom to move within the school grounds, but might be restricted from leaving school grounds and neighboring areas or entering certain Strategic Places without advance permission.

In times of high security alert, even persons who are considered lesser security risks may have to be excluded from certain Strategic Places. This will require the FBI to assign within the HSN a level of security risk to each person about whom some negative security information has been obtained.

The issue of profiling will surface immediately. While we must be sensitive to the issue of racial and ethnic profiling, there can be no doubt that it is justified and necessary in this instance to help prevent further terrorist acts. On the other hand, we must also make it clear to those persons who are the subject of ethnic or racial profiling that we regret any inconvenience they may be caused. They should quickly realize that they will ultimately benefit from the issuance of US IDs because, when they present a US ID, and they receive a security clearance, it will eliminate the suspicion which they currently face daily as a result of their physical appearance and ethnicity.

Many people, who by their physical appearance are difficult to distinguish from people in high risk groups, will benefit immediately from the issuance to them of a US ID, which when presented at any security check-point will indicate that they are not a security risk.

We must recognize that there is the strong probability that the people responsible for supplying information concerning security risks will be overly cautious or might carelessly or deliberately input information which unjustifiably designates a person as a security risk. Furthermore, we would instruct all persons delegated with the responsibility of determining whether certain information indicates that the cardholder poses a security risk, to be careful to note all information available in the HSN relating to the person whose identification is being checked. In some cases we can anticipate that they will be overzealous in determining that a security risk exists. It is clear, however, that the risk of not having a security system which relies on a US ID is so great, that we must be prepared to accept the difficulties it causes. A review system will have to be carefully designed to meet constitutional requirements of due process, and to ensure that errors will be corrected as quickly as practicable.

We must enable persons who are denied admission to a Strategic Place to request a review be undertaken of their security file. Such security review should be carried out promptly and, if practicable, within 60 days. This will require significant numbers of people to be hired by the FBI and trained to perform this very important task. They will have to be closely supervised to insure they perform their work with extreme care. Such review must be fair to and considerate of the rights of the people whose security information they are reviewing. Although restricting the movement of persons for security purposes raises serious Constitutional problems which must be dealt with by our courts, they are less serious than those relating to detention of persons by the FBI who are deemed a security risk which are already being dealt with.

Although we must expand the efforts to seal our borders, this is not the time to be dealing with the issue of illegal immigrants currently living in the US. Our efforts will be undermined if we do not make illegal immigrants eligible for US IDs. To encourage illegal immigrants to apply for a US ID we must make it clear that no one will be subject to deportation or loss of employment as a result of his or her application for a US ID other than those who have been involved with or who have aided and abetted terrorists or are subject to arrest for felonies unrelated to immigration issues.

Illegal immigrants must be guaranteed that in applying for the card FBI records will be reviewed and created solely for the purpose of determining any terrorist or felony connection. All persons must be assured that their personal information contained in the card will be used only to identify and restrict movement of terrorists and for law enforcement purposes unrelated to immigration matters. President Bush must convince all of our residents, whether they are here legally or not, that this time the government can be trusted to live up to its promise and that if they apply for a US ID their freedom of movement within the US will not be restricted.

PROTECTION OF
STRATEGIC PLACES

Issuing US IDs does not guarantee that all acts of terror will be prevented. We know that the FBI is making a concentrated effort to gather intelligence concerning terrorists to identify and take potential terrorists into custody. We do not know how thorough the effort is. It should probably be further expanded in conjunction with the issuance of US IDs. If they are not doing so, the FBI must as soon as practicable scrutinize all records of the last 10 years relating to visitor, student and work visas issued to persons of high risk groups, to identify them and trace the whereabouts of all of them who remain in the U.S., and do not apply for a US ID. We must thereafter determine if we should renew or change their status, detain, arrest or expel them.

The purpose of this section is to identify certain areas where we can improve our homeland security measures. Because of the complexity of the problem, it is intended merely to encourage consideration of certain steps which can and must be taken to protect our Strategic Places and our streets. Obviously our federal and state governments have security procedures in place and are taking steps to upgrade such procedures to protect many of our Strategic Places. We know that they have commenced taking action with respect to many of the items listed below. In many cases our effort needs to be expanded or improved.

No matter how diligent we are in linking security information to the US IDs we will be unable to rely solely on US IDs to identify and restrict the movement of terrorists and their weapons. Until we automate the process of checking US ID cards and support the checkpoints with security cameras, we can expect the individuals manning checkpoints will become lax because of lack of competence, negligence, laziness or boredom in utilizing the fingerprint and other verification equipment. We must also assume that there will be terrorists about whom we do not have any negative security information, who will either be issued a US ID or who will remain in hiding after gaining entry into the US and who do not apply for a US ID.

The FBI must avail itself of the media to conduct a meaningful campaign to elicit the assistance of all of our citizens and legal residents and law abiding illegal residents to identify and ferret out those who are planning to harm us. Local police departments, healthcare providers, airport and airline personnel and passengers, sellers of bomb-making products and hazardous materials and persons likely to come in contact with people of high risk groups, should be alerted to the important role that they may play in identifying terrorists before they carry out further acts within our country.

A hotline should be created and broadly advertised to enable anyone to anonymously report persons who they have reason to believe might be terrorists to a homeland security office or the FBI. People should be asked to report online, or in a manner which can be inputted into and analyzed by a computer, about persons who may have worked with, dated or befriended them who have moved into or unexpectedly moved out of their neighborhood within the past few years or may have been seen at a school, place of worship, place of work, social club, bar, restaurant or gym. We must seek the assistance of and offer funding for training of local law enforcement agencies and coordinate their efforts with the FBI, CIA and other federal intelligence agencies to round up and detain all of those who would commit acts of terror.

OTHER ACTIONS TO IMPROVE OUR HOMELAND SECURITY

The following is a list of other actions we can take to improve our homeland security:

* The Homeland Security Department should establish a homeland security force, as an elite armed force to work with the FBI, CIA, other security agencies, state national guards and local law enforcement and civil defense agencies.

* The homeland security force should be given primary responsibility based on instructions emanating from the FBI, which should continue in its role of attempting to locate and capture terrorists, to coordinate (i) restricting the movement of potential terrorists and (ii) guarding and restricting entry to Strategic Places and particularly places such as nuclear power plants which if attacked even if shut down could endanger the lives of millions of people.

* The homeland security force will need to have available to it and be responsible for distributing, on an as needed basis, cameras, electronic surveillance equipment, fencing, barricades and structures and sophisticated weaponry.

* Wherever practicable we must place security cameras in entrances and within and on the outside of Strategic Places, in entrances to our highways, in parking areas and in parks. The information received from cameras should be reviewed electronically by face recognition equipment and stored for designated periods of time which will vary by location, and be available for later access.

* Electronically controlled gates and buffer zones will have to be designed and installed to block attempts to break through security at certain Strategic Places and to aid in the capture of terrorists.

* We should have the homeland security force, policemen or firemen, routinely inspect all Strategic Places for the presence of bombs or hazardous gases or materials.

* We should have the homeland security officers randomly inspect briefcases and backpacks before boarding or during transit on buses, trains and boats and when entering or inside any of our Strategic Places. This will not prevent acts of suicide bombers, but will restrict the movement of hazardous materials and the placement of bombs within Strategic Places to be detonated remotely.

* We may have to prohibit the carrying of or inspect luggage or packages transported by train or bus in the same manner as we do at airports. New types of delivery services may have to be provided.

* To augment our effort to prevent entry of terrorists and weapons of mass destruction, we must seal the entire length of our borders and our shores. At a minimum this will require a more coordinated effort, a greater military presence, much more sophisticated electronic surveillance equipment and additional fencing.

* All ports should be fenced and no person arriving by ship should be permitted outside of the fenced area without a visa and US ID. Any services which the incoming sailors require will have to be provided within the fenced areas.

* In order to prevent illegal entry of individuals into our country by boat and to question the crew and obtain preliminary information relating to cargo, the Coast Guard should be equipped with vessels to enable it to guard our coastline and board and inspect while still at sea, all incoming ships and boats before they enter our ports or land on our shores.

* We are attempting to inspect containers and baggage entering this country from abroad, but as we know from the reported security breaches, we can do much better. Computerization of inspections should be expanded. Although inspecting the contents of all containers may be impossible, we should randomly have customs inspectors present when a container is packed and require such inspected containers to be sealed until after they pass US Customs. The move-

ment of all containers prior to entry into our country and until they reach their final destination should be carefully documented. Random inspections should take place at security checkpoints.

* Randomly inspecting cargo and parcels at checkpoints within our borders, another immense task, should be placed under the control of the homeland security force.

* The safety of nuclear power plants should be vastly improved. The perimeter of each plant should be protected by barricades and a strong military presence. We should add or upgrade electronic fencing and surveillance cameras, reinforce entrances and place defensive missiles around the power plant to intercept any incoming aircraft or missiles. The security clearances for all personnel should be regularly reviewed and all personnel should be closely monitored. We should also construct steel frames or towers which rise above such plants to prevent any aircraft or missile from making a direct hit. Systems should be designed to detect unusual activity and automatically shut the system down. We should also develop offsite capability to shut the plant down in an emergency.

* We may have to provide police or military escorts at all points in our oil, gas and hazardous products delivery systems and vastly increase security at oil refineries and oil, gas and hazardous materials storage facilities.

* We should consider installing a device which will enable a driver to deliberately and safely immobilize, until reversed by the homeland security force, oil or gas or hazardous materials delivery trucks so that they cannot be seized and turned into a weapon of mass destruction.

* We should apply gasoline mileage requirements to trucks and apply the law to existing vehicles. We should subsidize the replacement and elimination of low mileage vehicles to ameliorate the economic consequences.

* We should encourage our citizens to lower the thermostat in the winter at home and at work and reduce air conditioning usage wherever practicable.

* We must further subsidize the use of alternative energy sources.

* We should encourage additional oil storage tanks to be located throughout the country and away from structures to deal with potential short term shortages.

DEALING WITH FUTURE TERRORIST ATTACKS

We must be prepared to deal with any type of terrorist attack, whether it is in the form of a single event or is of a continuing nature. The following steps amongst others should be taken to deal with the possibility of future terrorist attacks:

* We should whenever we have the opportunity to do so increase the size of the national oil reserves. We must develop a better working relationship with our oil suppliers. We should increase our purchases to support the price of oil in times of surplus in exchange for promises from the producers to increase supply in times of shortages.

* Since the oil supply can be drastically reduced at any time, we must prior to the time that an emergency exists put into place a system to ration electricity, gasoline and heating oil, in a way to maximize the war effort and minimize even more severe negative effects on our economy and our comfort.

* We must develop contingency plans and fund programs for dealing with the after-effects of any type of terrorism that might strike us or countries that supply us with products or services.

* We must promptly assemble a team of qualified experts to consider the potential effects of war and future terrorist acts on all aspects of our productive capacity and demand for products and services. They must also assess the potential impact of the war on availability of raw materials, particularly oil and of foreign made products. We must not be dependent on supplies or production of any important product, from countries which might at any time be cut off. We should subsidize the development of the capacity to produce selected products to ensure that we will have the ability to produce them if the need arises.

* We must purchase and warehouse parts and equipment and train personnel to promptly repair or replace any section of our nation's infrastructure or our transportation or communication networks which might be damaged by future terrorist acts so that we will be prepared to limit the effect of potential disruptions.

* We must prepare for the eventuality that we may have to turn to some form of allocation of our resources and productive capacity to support our latest effort to defend our freedom. Now is the time to prepare for such an eventuality. We should be developing contingent plans to adopt price controls and rationing if shortages develop.

* We must consider tax credits or outright grants for companies to develop short and long term contingency plans and purchase back up facilities including standby power-generating equipment to be able to continue operations within hours or days, in the event that they are the direct or indirect subject of a terrorist attack.

* We must develop reliable backup systems for the Internet to guard against cyber terror. Merchants and credit card companies should develop alternative methods of payment if the current system is disrupted. Banks should be prepared to dispense cash at a customer's local branch using separate computer systems.

* We must take actions to enable our businesses to operate following a terrorist attack.

* We must consider the potential need for and develop plans to put into place debt moratoriums and subsidies to avoid defaults by companies in industries that are negatively impacted by shortages, rationing or loss of demand due to terrorist acts.

* We must be prepared to deal with contamination of our food or water supply.

* We must be prepared to limit the spread of disease.

* We must upgrade our inspections of food and water.

* We must electronically and remotely monitor air quality at thousands of locations.

* Adequate supplies of appropriate antibiotics should be available at hospitals and pharmacies throughout the country.

* We must either vaccinate everyone against smallpox or have adequate supplies available throughout the country and instructions as to how they will be administered.

* We should expand and upgrade our facilities to promptly analyze new chemical or biological weapons and develop the capacity to promptly deliver antidotes and vaccines.

* We must establish and test secure emergency TV and Internet sites.

* We should construct air pollution and radiation shelters, stocked with food and water, where feasible throughout our nation, including in office buildings,

armories, shopping malls, apartment houses, homes and vacation homes. They should be subsidized by tax credits.

* We must encourage all families to have available a portable radio and flashlights and adequate supplies of food, water, blankets, batteries and candles.

* Gas masks should be made available and we should be trained in their use.

* Potassium iodide tablets should be available for everyone.

* We must develop vaccines and treatments to control the damage which may result from the use of a biological weapon.

* We must consider steps to be taken to quarantine arriving plane or boat passengers for a period of time, if required in the future.

* We must train civil defense teams and conduct drills so that everyone knows what to do and how to evacuate an area and transport and treat the injured in the event of a bomb explosion or the use of a biological or chemical weapon.

* We must train special units to deal with cleanup operations following the attack by bombs and chemical or nuclear weapons.

* We must provide subsidies to state and local governments to enable them to train and equip policemen, firemen, National Guard and emergency medical professionals and volunteers to provide medical assistance and develop plans for emergency medical facilities if hospital emergency rooms become overburdened or unusable.

* We must be prepared to protect emergency workers from attack from terrorists.

* We must have standby power available wherever it may be needed.

* We must prepare for an attack on one or more hospitals.

DEALING WITH OUR ECONOMY-INVESTMENT AND MACROECONOMIC GAMES

THE IMPORTANCE OF OUR ECONOMY

Recognizing security as a first priority does not mean that the problems with our economy are not also of utmost importance. Except for the fact that we are at war, the economy would obviously be our top priority. It is of great urgency that we end the recession and return the economy to a course of sustainable growth. Our economy goes to the very essence of our way of life. A strong economy is also necessary to finance the large costs of war and will make us better able to withstand the financial impact of any future terrorist acts.

THE GOVERNMENT'S ROLE IN THE GAME OF MACROECONOMICS

There is virtual unanimity among economists that government plays a vital role in maintaining our country's growth and prosperity. There are widely diverse opinions among leading economists as to what actions the government should take at any time. Determining the actions which should be taken to maintain prosperity and growth in our economy is the game of macroeconomics. Like war, it is a very serious game which has a substantial impact on our lives.

When we talk of growth and prosperity we are generally referring to increases (or decreases) in our nations Gross Domestic Product ("GDP") which is the aggregate of the products and services produced in our country. GDP varies with the demand for products and services from individuals, businesses and governments on a worldwide basis. Such demand is based on hundreds of millions of separate decisions independently made. When our Government plays the game of macroeconomics it takes or fails to take actions which directly impact the economy and are designed to encourage individuals, businesses and governments worldwide to make decisions the totality of which, though made individually, will increase the aggregate demand for domestic products and services.

Since we have one worldwide marketplace, players of the game of macroeconomics must consider the effects which the spending decisions of foreign individuals, businesses and governments have on our GDP and of our actions on foreign economies. The economies of foreign countries grew with ours in the 1990s and they currently suffer similar problems resulting from overcapacity and insufficient demand. The game of macroeconomics is highly complex with each action affecting many others.

One might expect and it is generally true that a decision by our Government to lower interest rates or increase its domestic purchases will lead to an overall increase in demand and a tax cut will leave additional funds in the hands of the recipients of such tax cut and make it likely that they will increase their spending. One might also expect the opposite effect to follow increases in interest rates or decreases in government spending and tax increases. However, it is not that simple. For example, a reduction in interest rates lowers borrowing costs encouraging spending, but it also reduces interest income on savings which makes less interest income available to spend.

The aggregate short term and long term effect of the Federal Reserve Board's ("Fed") actions with respect to money supply and interest rates, of changes in tax rates and levels of government spending and the timing of the taking of such actions, impact many other factors to be considered when playing the game of macroeconomics. They include the government deficit, long and short term interest rates, the rate of inflation, savings rates, the level of capacity at which various industries are operating, the level of unemployment, the availability of raw materials, consumer confidence and spending, stock prices and business spending decisions relative to inventory levels, research and development, hiring and firing of employees, capital expenditures and sales and marketing expenses. In turn, all of these factors have an affect on each other. Macroeconomic planning is also impacted by the effects on the worldwide economy of natural disasters, political changes and acts of war. It is no wonder that economists carefully study all the leading economic indicators and events and still disagree as to what actions should be taken in playing the game.

Before we can determine what further steps our Government should take now in playing the game of macroeconomics to return our economy to prosperity, we should review the causes of our economy reaching its currently perilous condition. During the 1990s the very nature of the free enterprise system and of our securities' markets inevitably created excesses which were followed by an abrupt reversal in our economy, as has occurred often in our nation's history. It was widely known, by people who understand business cycles, that a correction in the stock market and our economy was long overdue. However, the stock market and the economy had become so overheated that the underlying problems were masked. Because our stock market and our economy reached such lofty levels, the decline which followed was steeper than usual.

The fraud and greed of corporate executives, accountants, banks and investment bankers is daily blamed in the never-ending exposes in our newspapers, magazines and on TV as the reason for the enormous $7 trillion decline in stock market values. Fraud and greed are only a part of the whole picture. Bad investment decisions, poor business judgment, overexpansion, the effects of competition and the events of Sept 11, all contributed to the collapse. Once the decline began, margin liquidations, stop loss orders, sales by chart theory followers, program selling, short selling, mutual fund redemptions and selling by investors and mutual funds who for any number of reasons preferred to reduce or liquidate their holdings, all contributed to drive stock prices lower. Stock index funds, which are fully invested at all times and must sell the underlying shares to pay for redemptions, have been heavily redeemed in the past three years. Program selling has contributed to the volume and speed of trading and led to increased volatility.

As discussed below, all of the above factors, many of which have no relationship to the underlying value of the securities being bought and sold, have a profound effect on the stock market. The negative impact of the above factors could have been limited by government enforcement of the laws and rules which regulate businesses and the securities' markets and by making changes in such rules and regulations to meet changing circumstances. Our presidents and their economic advisors, the Securities and Exchange Commission ("SEC"), the Fed and Congress and so many other people with the responsibility of enforcing and improving our laws and rules, failed miserably in meeting their responsibilities. To make matters worse, they all deny their own responsibility and do not seem to be aware of many of the reasons which caused the stock market collapse, or the gravity of the risks which may impact our economy in the coming months and years.

The following pages attempt to explain factors which should be considered by our Government before making its next moves in the game of macroeconomics. These factors help to explain our sustained growth over a long period of time leading to excessive increases in securities prices and overly aggressive and sometimes mindless risk taking by businesses and the underlying causes of the precipitous decline in stock prices and the contraction of our economy when the bubble finally burst. They explore the depth of the wounds which our economy has suffered and attempt to explain the reasons why, if left alone, our economy and stock prices are unlikely to recover at a desirable rate, if at all, and why we face a serious risk of entering into a deflationary spiral. They also substantiate the argument that increased government spending, which is required for our homeland defense, is also desirable to spur our economic recovery.

THE GROWTH OF THE ECONOMY DURING THE 1990S AND THE INCREASE IN THE VALUE OF SECURITIES

We begin with a review of events which materially impacted and propelled the growth and prosperity in the 90s. The long period of growth and prosperity began slowly and innocuously as various events took place. The Fed began to lower interest rates, the capacity of computers grew exponentially, software development enhanced the usefulness of computers and the Internet came into being and spawned a new growth industry. The new technologies permitted us to perform certain tasks in new ways and increased worker productivity leading to increased profits and non-inflationary growth. The worldwide emergence of cell phones, and the growth in use of the Internet generated explosive growth in the communications industry. The Clinton administration which had inherited the stimulus resulting from the war against Iraq, the cost of which had been reimbursed in large part by Saudi Arabia, championed a tax increase which proved to be stimulative in the aggregate because it led to a drop in interest rates which accelerated the growth already under way. Thereafter, it effectively put the economy on automatic pilot.

Spectacular advances in technology brought about by a new generation of entrepreneurs were the core of our economic expansion. Trillions of dollars of wealth was created during a period of seven or eight years principally as a result of the creation and rapid growth of technology, communication, biotech and Internet entities and the rapid growth of energy trading companies which precipitated worldwide growth. Investors and mutual funds poured billions of dollars into the securities of these entities and watched their market value soar. Hundreds of exceptional products and services were developed. Newly formed enterprises flush with cash hired highly compensated executives and employees, and granted them generous stock options to give them the incentive to be productive. They created an infrastructure, rented space, bought high tech products and parts and developed and marketed new products and services.

The shares of these entities were so attractive that investors were anxious to add them to their holdings. They greatly expanded their purchasing power by buying on margin. Funds poured from accounts set aside for retirement, individual savings accounts, pensions funds, profit sharing plans and corporate cash reserves into purchases of securities. Investments in mutual funds soared and they in turn purchased hundreds of billions of dollars worth of shares of stock. It seemed that everyone wanted to participate in the unlimited growth of American business. Banks, investment bankers and brokerages generated substantial profits. They went public and their share prices soared.

The share prices of many of the stock market leaders such as GE and IBM started a long continuous rise. New stock market star performers like Microsoft, Cisco, Intel, eBay, Yahoo, AOL, Sun Microsystems, Oracle, Dell, Enron, World-Com, Global Crossing, Adelphia and Tyco and hundreds of other entities appeared almost daily. The growing companies had large capital needs to finance their dynamic expansion. Investment bankers seized the opportunity and underwrote ever increasing equity and debt offerings. The success of the offerings led to financing of other entities in the growth industries which were also successful. Banks extended loans to these entities for working capital and expansion. Imaginative derivatives of all types were introduced and generated large profits for investors and investment bankers. Almost anyone with an idea for an Internet business and an attractive business plan could raise tens of millions of dollars. Success bred success. Investors who bought shares of companies in the growth industries were rewarded with large paper profits. With a minimum of luck and effort, it was easy to get rich quickly.

The interplay between stock prices and the economy fueled the rise of both. As the economy expanded, companies expanded their work forces, spent on R&D and invested in plant and equipment and technology, all of which generated further revenue and earnings increases for other companies and had a multiplier effect as the spending spread throughout the economy. Stock prices soared as revenues and earnings grew and investors became rich and watched their retirement savings grow exponentially. Companies paid large salaries and bonuses and granted stock options, particularly to management who found ways to obtain the largest number of options and often, exorbitant salaries and bonuses. Few stockholders complained while stock prices went up. The boom spread to other industries as the newly founded companies and their highly paid employees spent the funds they received. The rising stock prices and high interest rates generated increases in the value of pension funds resulting in many of them being over funded. As a result companies were able to reduce their pension contributions and increase their earnings.

The US Government was a principal beneficiary as income and capital gains tax collections soared. State tax revenues grew and state tax rates were reduced giving further purchasing power to consumers. Although government spending grew, Federal deficits turned into large surpluses, government debt was retired and interest rates declined. It was easy for our Government to make the right moves in the game of macroeconomics.

The rapidly growing GDP fueled more growth in what appeared to be a never-ending growth spiral. We seemed to have a new formula for playing the game of macroeconomics. Price earnings ratios of companies included in the major market indexes and those listed on NASDAQ rose to record levels to reflect the expected future growth of American industry. In some instances shares of startup companies sold at 100 times the future earnings that analysts dreamed about, but were disconnected from reality. As stock prices rose, a new breed of securities analysts, most of them never having observed a recession, became adept at adjusting price earnings ratios to eliminate acquisition and restructuring costs and fostered new valuation methods for start-up companies, many of which were only in the process of designing and developing unproven products for use on the Internet.

The risks of leverage were ignored. Who cared anyway, since the market price of so many stocks doubled and doubled again and then kept going up. There was a large list of companies hitting new highs published daily. Analysts were paid big salaries for recommending almost anything. It didn't matter that their reasoning was often flawed or that they had a conflict of interest because they worked for the company's investment banker. Investors were more concerned with the benefit which the issuer might get from its association with the investment banker. For many if not most investors, particularly young investors who had never experienced a downturn, the underlying value of the business meant nothing or very little. If you waited to jump on the bandwagon and purchase shares of the rising stars, you missed an opportunity. But, since almost everything was going up, it was never too late to capitalize on the next stock price rise.

One unsophisticated investor after another was drawn into the market and the value of their investments grew materially. Even sophisticated investors jumped on the bandwagon. They observed the benefits the economy was deriving from the euphoria and the wealth effect and sought to capitalize by buying overpriced issues driving the price still higher. Many investors were getting rich purchasing on margin which greatly increased their purchasing power and by buying new issues which doubled and tripled within days of the offering. Few investors cashed out or paid attention to forecasters of doom.

Before we look at the reasons this economic environment came to an end, it is important to review the role that margin buying, the sale of new issues and short selling each contributed to the exaggerated highs in the market indexes as they often have throughout our history.

PURCHASING ON MARGIN

The use of margin during the 1990s added many billions of dollars to the purchasing power of investors. A hypothetical example of the effects of margin buying on the price of securities is as follows.

Suppose an investor buys a marginable security for $25,000 which doubles in value to $50,000. There were many such securities in the 90s. His broker then calls to recommend a new purchase and he says he has no additional funds to add to his account. His broker says that is not a problem as he now has $50,000 of purchasing power (he had $25,000 in additional purchasing power when he opened the account) if he buys at 50% margin. He therefore buys more of the same or another security for $50,000 leaving him with $100,000 of securities and the same equity of $50,000. The portfolio doubles again leaving him with an equity of $150,000 and purchasing power without adding new funds of $100,000. He again takes full advantage of his purchasing power and purchases additional shares and now has portfolio of $300,000. Suppose it doubles again. He now has $600,000 worth of securities and an equity of $450,000. Note that if his original $25,000 investment had doubled three times without any margin purchases, he would have had an account with a value of $200,000. He then makes additional stock purchases using his $300,000 of additional purchasing power raising his loan to $450,000. When the portfolio doubles again it is worth $1,800,000 and he has an equity of $1,350,000. Without using margin his account would be worth $400,000. He then has additional purchasing power of $900,000. He feels rich and does not hesitate to purchase additional securities to bring his portfolio to $2,700,000 and his margin loan to $1,350,000. The size of the debit balance seems irrelevant. He is a millionaire and his wealth is increasing.

It is no wonder NASDAQ prices soared. Technology and Internet companies were in favor. This one hypothetical investor was able to make aggregate purchases of $1,325,000 based on an initial investment of $25,000 and, if he wished, without selling any of the shares he had purchased. He may have achieved the same result even if his investments had not been as successful if he had increased his purchasing power by adding additional funds along the way. Although the above described trading account is hypothetical, there were many investors who invested in stocks such as Microsoft, Cisco, Yahoo and Intel and achieved even greater growth in the value of their portfolio by utilizing margin to parlay their gains as stock prices soared in the 90s. Some might argue that the investor has benefitted from margin purchases and no one has been injured. Many young investors who were tuned in to the growth in technology took advantage of margin to multiply their profits, without the faintest understanding of the risks and dangers of buying on margin. If their brokers understood the risk they probably didn't bother to tell them.

THE NEW ISSUE GAME

The new issue market, which created instant wealth and contributed to the growing investor excitement and euphoria, also contributed to the market rise. It is a game which has for many years been a phenomenon unto itself. The new issue game begins with the lead underwriter locating and entering into a letter of intent with an issuer. The process is highly competitive. The issuers seek to raise the maximum amount of capital with the minimum amount of dilution possible. Since the lead underwriter generally continues as your investment banker after the offering, management's relationships with the investment banker prior to offering or the reputation of the investment banker often affect the decision. Every underwriter seeks to set up a schedule of offerings which are of the type currently in favor with investors.

While the offering documents are prepared and go through an SEC review, the underwriting syndicate is formed and the participating brokers and dealers line up prospective customers. When placing the shares which an underwriter or dealer has been allotted in the offering, the brokers working for the underwriters and dealers are allocated a number of the shares being offered and in turn determine which of their customers will be given the opportunity to subscribe to the offering and the number of shares which will be available for them. Investment bankers dole out shares of new issues to their best customers. They generally try to avoid customers who have previously dumped the last issue at or shortly after the commencement of trading unless they are important customers whom they elect to reward.

The press and government officials are now questioning the propriety, even though it was done openly, of underwriters giving allocations of new issues to executives and financial officers of potential issuers to enable them to line up a future offering or customers or potential customers in an attempt to obtain or retain their investment banking business. Few people complained that these executives and financial officers were benefitting from the corporate opportunities of their employers.

Once the new issue market heats up, a buying frenzy develops and almost all issues begin trading at prices substantially above the offering price. Investors place orders to purchase as many shares as they can get of each issue, subject only to the limits of their buying power. They tell their friends to buy on the offering or in the after-market. Since investors, even sophisticated investors, do not care what shares they are buying as long as they go up immediately, they rarely take more than a casual look at or rely upon the prospectus. If they notice the pages of risk factors, they rarely pay attention to them. Some didn't ask and others didn't understand the nature of the business.

Many customers are disappointed with their allocation. In fact when the market becomes heated up, less important customers are offered the opportunity to purchase only a small number or no shares on the offering. However, since they and their broker feel certain that the stock will rise quickly in the after-market the broker discusses the purchase of shares in the after-market with such customers. He lines up after-market orders to be placed the day the stock opens for trading. Investors try to guess where the stock will open so that they can purchase at the lowest price before the stock runs up further.

Some brokers are now being accused of illegally requiring customers to place an after-market order as a condition of getting an allocation of a new issue, but in a "hot" new issue market that was totally unnecessary. We must distinguish between the limited number of brokers who required purchases in the after-market and those who recommended such purchases. The former is illegal and the latter is not only appropriate but also diligent in some circumstances. Brokers who violated the law were in most cases acting contrary to their employer's rules and without its knowledge.

The reason that such a high percentage of new issues rise rapidly during periods that there is a "hot" new issue market is easily explained. They go up because as noted above, investors who can't get all the shares they want in the initial offering, place orders to buy when the trading commences which greatly exceed the very limited number of shares offered for resale. This occurs because the process of selling new issues and the initial after-market activity becomes a game and the people who buy new issues play by the unspoken and unwritten rule of the game which might be called the "no resale" rule, namely, if you get an allocation of shares you do not sell new issues at or shortly after the offering.

Other factors limit the resale of new issues. There is a standard provision in the Agreement Among Underwriters which allows the lead underwriter to cause underwriters whose customers sell their shares during the offering period, to repurchase such shares which the lead underwriter acquires while stabilizing the market. Underwriters therefore have a good reason to place the shares with investors who will not sell them for a period of time. The float is limited because sales by insiders is limited under Rule 144 promulgated by the SEC. Rule 144, which regulates resales of restricted securities, prohibits sales of unregistered securities for a 90 day period after an initial public offering and the underwriters generally prevent insiders from selling for a period of six months or more. Of course, high income investors are also locked in by the ordinary income tax rate on short-term gains.

It is not unusual for the players to rely on their brokers to tell them when to sell and take their profit. Brokers find it difficult to recommend selling new issues even if they go to prices beyond their expectations because they must determine which customer they will call first and sales tend to drive the stock down. As a result brokers often fail to remind customers to sell. They generally call only to tell how your portfolio has increased in value or to extend an invitation to play golf or attend a sporting event or concert or to discuss your purchase of the next new issue.

The new issue game had so many players in the 1990s that they were able to ignore the "no resale" rule and pay no attention when customers sold to realize their gains. But who wanted to sell since so many of the new issues kept going up? Many people, watching the explosive growth of the Internet, believed that we were only at the beginning of the cyberspace revolution and that the pie in the sky projections based on the potential unlimited growth of the Internet were attainable. Underwriters sought out issuers which were formed to develop computer software, Internet related products, telecommunications products, biotechnology products and other technology entities and almost all the IPOs were an instant success.

Wealth was created instantly which over time led to additional margin buying power which, as noted above, drove the prices of securities higher across the board. During the 1990s the new issue market became so frantic that underwriters sought out potential issuers who had any plausible idea for a dot com business and an attractive-looking but not necessarily well-reasoned business plan, and raised large sums of money for them when they were merely start-ups. In order for the investment bankers to maintain their earnings growth they underwrote shares of an increasing number of issuers with marginal prospects. So much paper wealth was being created instantly that people left secure jobs in all types of occupations, including, engineers, accountants and lawyers, to become founders, equity owners and employees of these unproven companies. Companies were formed to provide seed capital to newly formed entities.

The offerings had certain things in common. The investment bankers were making large underwriting fees and commissions, equity participations and consulting fees and the share prices were skyrocketing in value immediately upon the commencement of trading. Lawyers and accountants were being paid large fees.

SHORT SELLING IN A RISING MARKET

While short selling may have been expected to impede the rise in price of some securities, it often had the opposite effect. Short sellers, who thought the price of a security was excessive and sold short, got squeezed when the price of the stock continued to rise and panicked or were unable to meet margin calls and were forced to cover, further adding to price increases. During the 1990s it was not unusual for the price of a stock to soar when large short positions relative to the average daily trading volume were reported when investors placed buy orders and short sellers rushed in to cover their positions. It was all part of the investment game.

THE INEVITABLE RESULT

With all these factors driving securities prices upward, what went wrong? As the long period of expansion continued underwriters sought out ever more speculative entities to add to their underwriting backlogs. During the period of growth investment banking companies had been mesmerized by attractive business plans which talked about new products and technologies that sounded attractive. They dispensed billions of dollars to entities with little or no track record to enable them to develop or market new products or expand by acquisition or through capital investments in ill conceived or unproven business ventures.

The legislated separation of banks and investment banks was eliminated, first by permitting banks to use loopholes to get around the law, and then with the repeal, with little opposition, of the Glass Steagall Act. That act had prohibited banks, since the days of the Great Depression, from the risks and conflicts which result from their being in the investment banking business. The banks had argued that they needed to establish investment banking divisions in order to remain competitive in the global marketplace. Many large banks soon bought investment banking companies, often at substantial premiums over inflated market prices.

Banks, investment bankers and aggressively managed companies established divisions to become involved as partners or investors in many of the high risk technology, communications and energy trading ventures. The saving and loan fiasco was forgotten. The Fed's regulation of risk taking by banks was woefully inadequate.

In fairness, although they may have been blinded by the large investment banking fees they were receiving, most of the people involved probably believed that the ventures they were financing would be successful and that they were participants in brilliantly conceived and perfectly legal practices which had been reviewed and approved by the lawyers and accountants. Such practices were often described in the often lengthy and difficult to understand footnotes of the company's financial statements. Where possible, the bank's transactions were fully hedged or insured to guarantee profitability. However, the banks and investment bankers appear to have been unconcerned that the transactions were getting larger and more convoluted and often had no real business purpose except to keep debt off the balance sheet or increase short term profits for one or more of the players. Banks and investment bankers maximized short term profits financing high risk ventures, which led to large salaries for their executives and highly educated but often inexperienced employees.

During the meteoric rise investment bankers and investors had greedily overlooked or ignored the fact that many of these Internet and telecommunications companies were formed to develop similar types of products or products which were never fully developed or marketed properly, and did not gain market acceptance. A substantial portion of the funds raised in the communications and other high tech industries were spent developing, licensing and acquiring, at increasingly higher cost, capacity which turned out to be excess capacity. One of the vagaries of an open market system is that unless one has patent or copyright protection or proprietary knowhow competitors, even those which make bad business decisions, can offer destructive competition. The problem is exacerbated in a computerized world where it is difficult to protect one's intellectual property from a competitor who engages in reverse engineering.

Large investments were made in ventures based on unrealistic cost and revenue projections. Some products became outmoded in a short time period as technological advances occurred at an ever faster rate. Internet companies paid marketing fees to other internet companies for introducing potential customers to their site even if they failed to purchase anything or pay a service fee. Many Internet companies found that they could not charge for services which their competitors gave away for free.

The inevitable occurred as it had in all prior hot new issue markets. Many of the projections and dreams were not realized for a variety of reasons including flawed business plans, competitive factors, poor management and risks which had been disclosed in the prospectus, but had been ignored by the investment bankers, analysts and investors. The day of reckoning arrived for one company after another. Some of the ill-conceived, underfunded or poorly managed companies failed to meet their development schedules or revenue projections and simply ran out of money.

As had been the case in past new issue markets and in investing in securities in general, timing is essential. The price of many new issues which had soared shortly after the issuer went public, sold substantially below the initial offering price 3 to 5 years after the offering. Investors who sold their shares as the prices climbed made large profits. Those who held on to such issues particularly those who purchased at a premium in the after-market, sustained losses.

The interplay between the stock market and the economy surfaced again. This time in reverse as falling stock prices impacted business credit worthiness and spending decisions. Companies that had gone back to their investment bankers from time to time to raise additional capital at increasing pre-money valuations and spent or even squandered whatever they were given on items such as excessive salaries or unproductive marketing and R&D expenditures expenses, found that the well had run dry. They could not raise additional capital at any price and they looked to merge or sell their assets or simply folded and closed their doors and their stock prices tanked.

Many of their employees, who had been millionaires on paper for a limited period of time, found themselves with worthless securities and unemployed. They sought other business opportunities or jobs which became more and more difficult as the decline accelerated. Other companies had adequate capital, at least for the short run, but failed to meet revenue or earnings projections and their stock prices went into steep declines.

Some companies survived by reorganizing to conserve their remaining cash or by getting credit from manufacturers who sought to increase sales revenues. Some of our most successful technology companies which had been the suppliers of and had in some cases extended credit to such companies suddenly found themselves with bad debts, reduced sales and large overcapacity compounded by the fact that almost new state of the art equipment was available for resale, at a large discount.

The malady spread throughout the dot coms and Internet companies. Their stock prices which had soared to unrealistic levels also began to decline. Companies which had joined in the festivities while share prices were rising, and had increased profits by investing in the dot coms and Internet entities, found themselves hit with losses as the prices of their investments declined. The air came out of the dot com and Internet balloon, slowly at first and then at an accelerated pace. Investors who were heavily invested in dot coms and Internet stocks watched as the value of their portfolio declined and losses began to appear on their brokerage statements. Initially few investors sold. Some had great confidence and an emotional attachment to the leading technology companies which had earned them large profits. Others were just slow to react.

Furthermore, the decline in interest rates during 2001 left many unsophisticated people who were living off their interest income with a dilemma. Either they had to begin to spend out of principal or they had to find alternative investments. A large number of so-called financial experts advised that equities offered the best opportunity for a long-term return on capital. They opined that the stock market which had declined from its highs looked poised for a recovery. Many investors withdrew cash from their bank accounts or used cash in their IRAs to purchase securities. Their purchases steadied the market for a while but, except for an occasional short-lived rally, the recovery did not come. The market averages began a long decline.

The decline in securities prices of the failed entities and their suppliers precipitated the adverse effects which margin liquidations, stop loss orders, chart theories, short selling, tax selling and the collapse of the new issue market, always have and have had in the past three years, in accelerating and deepening the decline in falling markets.

MARGIN LIQUIDATIONS

The reason that margin buying accelerates the decline in falling markets results from the fact that the margin investor owns more securities and the same percentage decline results in a larger aggregate dollar decline than would be sustained without the leverage. Maximizing margin purchases is a form of gambling. It is like doubling up every time you have a winning bet at a casino and failing to take any chips off the table when playing craps or blackjack. It is inevitable that eventually you will lose once and be wiped out. In the case of margin buying the leverage compounds the decline in the value of your account when the market declines.

Utilizing full margin at all times makes your portfolio the equivalent of a house of cards. As soon as your portfolio declines 20-25% from the point where you were fully extended on margin, the dark clouds begin to roll in. In the above hypothetical example a 25% decline from $2,700,000 reduces your portfolio to a value of $2,025,000 and your equity to $675,000 and the loan remains constant at $1,350,000. Although you equity is still substantial, it only takes a relatively minor further slide to reduce your portfolio to a value of $1,800,000 and an equity of $450,000 the point below which your broker is required to give you a margin call requiring you to add cash or securities to your portfolio. If you fail to do so the broker must sell sufficient securities to bring your account within the 25% equity requirement.

Of course, as the value of your portfolio declines further you will receive additional margin calls. It is an old adage on the "Street" that "You sell securities which reduce the loan to meet margin calls rather than adding new funds." The theory behind the adage is that if the market continues to decline you will eventually be unable to meet margin calls and will have to sell anyway. Needless to say that once a substantial number of investors receive margin calls and liquidate securities they precipitate a decline which results in further margin calls in the accounts of other investors. If the decline continues it will set off a further margin call in the investor's account.

When the market goes into a steep decline even investors who at the peak value of their portfolio had margin loans of only 25% (or even less) of the value of their accounts may eventually face margin calls. It is not unusual for investors who get caught in a spiral of margin liquidations to lose everything or even wind up with a debit balance in their account which is a debt to the broker. The broker will often dump your positions in a rapidly falling market at a drastically reduced bid price to avoid your account going underwater, because if you can't meet your margin obligation, the broker suffers the loss.

It is clear that the theoretical investor in the above example would have been better off if he had reduced the percentage of his margin loan as prices rose or even after they began to fall, to reduce the effect which might result from a market decline. However, many investors didn't understand the risk of buying on margin until after they began to receive margin calls.

Investors who buy on tips from friends, rumors, or on broker's or analyst's recommendations, often pay no attention to the changing business prospects or financial fundamentals of the companies they hold shares in. They may think about selling, but often they procrastinate and take no action. The source that told them to buy rarely recommends sale, and sometimes is precluded from doing so because of inside information constraints. The tipster may have forgotten he told you to buy the stock. When you ask him what action he is planning to take with respect to the stock he may even reply that he sold it a long time ago.

Human emotions are not helpful when investing in securities. The thought process of a typical investor might have gone something like this: The investor was confident at the top of the market, but began to question whether he should have sold after a 10% decline. When the portfolio declined another 10%, he thought to himself that he should have sold some of his shares at the top, and would sell on the first rally. If it rallied he felt better and waited till it got back to the high price which was often not reached or if it was reached he waited for it to go higher. If he was on full margin when it declined again and the drop reached 30%, he was in a state of panic and either sold or hoped for a recovery. As noted above his equity had been decimated by the 30% drop. He had all the problems faced by investors who are about to receive a margin call.

If he had only a small debit balance when the market declined by 30%, he generally decided he would sell if it recovered 10% or so. When the decline reached 40% he began to realize that he didn't understand what his securities were really worth, but felt certain that a rally was coming. When the decline reached 50% he felt that a rally was more likely and planned to sell on the rally. At 60% he was disgusted with himself and everyone he could think of to blame for the decline and questioned whether he should sell to keep what he had left. Generally he would procrastinate and decide to ride it out. He often decided to sell when it was down 70% or 80% depending on his own personal or family needs. He may have bailed out as the decline reached 90%. He may even have decided to go down with the ship.

He may have realized somewhere along the way, that he could understand why the share prices of some dot coms and Internet companies had declined and many had gone out of business. However, he probably didn't understand why the major technology companies had been so devastated until he realized that even the best technology companies had been overpriced and were being hurt by the dot com and Internet debacle and that in a falling stock market, the stock price of even the best companies decline. By then it was too late.

THE FAILURE TO RAISE MARGIN REQUIREMENTS

When we look back we see that our Fed chairman had recognized the "irrational exuberance" but, other than coin the phrase, did little to limit it. Perhaps he didn't want to be accused of killing the "Golden Goose" by taking an action which might cause the market to go down. Both Democrats and Republicans paid little attention to the economy except to claim credit for its strength. They relied on the Fed and the SEC, but failed to give the SEC the funding it needed. They were more concerned with supporting special interest groups which were large campaign contributors or were employers in their own state. They spent a large portion of their time fund raising and debating the issues which they felt would yield them votes, such as education, social security, prescription drugs, abortion, school prayer and vouchers and gun control.

In the past the Federal Reserve Board which regulates the permissible rate of margin, has raised margin requirements in rising markets to limit purchasing power and lower margin rates in falling markets to increase purchasing power. By raising margin requirements for investors making purchases in rising markets purchasing power is immediately reduced. For example if you have $150,000 of securities and $50,000 of debt, the $50,000 of purchasing power which you had at 50% margin disappears at 70% margin. It is readily apparent from the above example that if margin rates are lowered from 70% to 50% immediate purchasing power is created in accounts with more than 50% equity. By failing to raise margin rates as the prices of securities soared the Federal Reserve Board missed an opportunity to reduce the "irrational exuberance" of investors and left itself without the opportunity which it has had in past downturns to lower margin rates (although doing so creates added risk and may be a questionable action to take) to increase buying power to stimulate securities purchases.

Had the margin rates been raised to 75% or even 100% while market prices were soaring, substantial purchasing power would have been instantly eliminated which would have slowed the market's excessive rise, and the risk of future margin liquidations would have been reduced. Some margin purchasers whose portfolios had a run-up and then fell precipitously may still have seen their accounts liquidated even if their margin use had been limited to a smaller percentage than the 50% limit. Others would have survived the market decline without being liquidated or would have been in a better position to liquidate their portfolios and pay off their margin balance while they still had substantial equity in their accounts.

As is always the case in a falling stock market, some margin investors at every level of the decline, find themselves in a position where their accounts will be liquidated if there is a further drop in value of their portfolio or as the debit increases because of the interest which is accruing. Investors who have no margin debt can elect to ride out the decline and wait for a recovery. The Fed made a serious blunder in playing the game of macroeconomics by not raising the margin rate years before speculation got out of hand. Some brokers reduced the margin risk for themselves and customers, by raising their own margin requirements on certain securities or large positions in one stock. However, because of the unprecedented decline in technology stocks which ensued, this often proved inadequate to protect high risk investors even if their overall margin debts were limited to approximately 30% or 35 % at the top of the market.

BEAR RAIDS BY SHORT SELLERS

Short sales also destabilize falling markets since short sellers who have profited from declining prices have increased equity, enabling them to increase their short positions thereby impeding an upturn. A hypothetical example of how the game of short selling puts downward pressure on stock prices despite the rule that you can only sell short following an up tick follows. Suppose a company has reported disappointing earnings or has announced that it has uncovered a fraud and will restate its earnings. Although the market price may have dropped precipitously, let us assume that a number of short sellers acting separately, including large hedge funds, decide that there is a likelihood that the company will be the subject of further negative press, earnings declines, class action litigation, regulatory investigations, credit rating reductions or loan defaults. They know that investors are highly nervous and tend to panic if the stock prices of companies receiving negative publicity keep declining. They know that every time such a security makes a new low, additional margin sales may be precipitated.

Short sellers, like vultures, pray on the wounded. They swoop in to attack by selling short on each uptick the shares of almost any company which makes a negative disclosure. Like the robber barons of the late Nineteenth Century, they gamble that before they cover their short position the share price will decline precipitously. They wait for the press to dramatically report and then rehash every detail of wrongdoing. They know that a declining stock price and negative disclosures may affect credit ratings and cause concern among the company's creditors which may lead to a liquidity crisis. It seems that everyone wants to kick a company which is down. Existing stockholders unload positions knowing that other investors are likely to panic or incur margin calls, that chart theorists will interpret a sell signal and that short sellers will impede a recovery in the share price. Potential buyers become discouraged or frightened and wait on the sidelines for signs that a rally is underway before buying. Under such conditions, the market goes down precipitating all the other negative factors affecting the securities markets which lead to further declines.

Short sellers must comply with the uptick rule adopted in the 1930s to prevent bear raids, but that rule has been flawed since its inception. It does not prevent short sellers from playing the game by selling large numbers of shares precluding a price rise. Thus, if a stock sells at $42.25 and then $42.30 they can sell unlimited amounts of shares at $42.30. If it then drops to $42 and has a sale at $42.05, they can sell an unlimited number of shares short at $42.05. In weak markets spreads between the bid and ask often widen. Downticks are common as a nervous seller hits the bid or there is a margin liquidation at the bid price. Before long that same stock is trading at $37.75, $36.66, $35.50 and then $34.67 and may not have not had two consecutive upticks during the period of decline.

By being prepared to short large quantities, short sellers prevent a rally in the stock price, until buyers come along to purchase all the shares that short sellers are prepared to sell or until enough short sellers sense a recovery coming and make purchases to cover their short positions. In a weak market of the type which existed during the last three years, which followed stocks reaching unprecedented and excessive highs, this can be after the stock price has declined eighty or ninety percent. Even if a rally develops fueled by the covering of short positions which temporarily stems the slide, the next piece of bad news causes a new round of selling and brings in new shorts. The result is that the share price cascades downward again. In many cases the precipitous decline in the share price which is exaggerated by short selling leads to adverse business consequences for the company involved when the concerns of their lenders are elevated.

One might argue that when the stock goes down it will be more attractive to investors or that trading volume is so large that short selling cannot prevent a stock from recovering. However, large amounts have been placed in hedge funds by sophisticated investors and a large number of traders have discovered the profitability of shorting in a falling market. Many investors who profited by following the crowd in the rising market are now finding it profitable to join the short sellers.

Even though it may be difficult to prove manipulative intent, the SEC should be investigating short selling practices to determine if bear raids have occurred in selected securities. This will at least discourage attempts to manipulate the stock market downward.

Other than the fact that we have long permitted short sales, we might ask why you should be permitted to sell securities you do not own in the hope that you can buy them back cheaper. Securities are not like commodities where short positions can be used for hedging purposes to lock in a sale price for farmers and miners in advance of their getting their product, currently being grown or mined, to market. Short positions may be used to hedge other positions, but the alternative is to sell the other positions. Even though brokerages profit from the fees they receive from their stock loan departments, a strong argument can be made for prohibiting short selling entirely. At the very least serious consideration should be given to forbidding short selling when a security is selling for less than 60% or 50% of its 24 month high. We might also prohibit short selling after a predetermined percentage drop in one or more of the major market indexes. This would tend to eliminate bear raids.

THE END OF THE NEW ISSUE GAME

As soon as the market began declining, investors stopped placing orders to buy shares at a premium in the after-market and new issues began to trade at or near the initial offering price. Without instant profits investors stopped playing the new issue game and the new issue market came to a standstill. It became almost impossible for start-up companies and even some established companies which found themselves in need of capital, to go to the new issue market for financing.

The new issue mania which had fueled the stock market exuberance worked in reverse as the instant profits from new issues turned into losses aggregating hundreds of billions of dollars for the investors who had held on to the shares of IPOs or who bought them in the after-market. Many of the investors were forced to sell to meet margin calls. Others decided to sell which in turn led to further price declines since there were few buyers.

OTHER SELLERS

When financial news turns negative and the stock market decline accelerates, mutual funds often find themselves facing net redemptions. In the case of index funds which remain fully invested they must sell the underlying shares to finance the redemptions.

Some investors who wish to protect their gains or limit their losses place stop loss orders for such purpose. Chart theorists also determine a point in a falling market at which they will sell their position in a stock. There are numerous types of chart theories which rely on graphs of movements of stock prices and indexes over differing periods of time which are interpreted as buy or sell signals. Many investors who use stop loss orders are cognizant of chart theories and place stop loss orders to protect themselves from the drop which may occur when chart theorists observe a sell signal. As the market declines, forced margin selling, stop loss orders, mutual fund redemptions and sales by followers of chart theory tend to interact to accelerate the drop. It's all part of the game of investing.

THE END OF A BUSINESS CYCLE

The new issue market had funded some of the great success stories of the 90s but also funded too many poorly conceived or managed and now failed ventures some of which went bankrupt. It had created high paying jobs now lost, and had stimulated unsustainable product and investment demand which in turn had led to over-expanded manufacturing capacity for technological products. Many thousands of jobs in the investment banking and brokerage industry, which were created during the hot new issue market, have been lost.

Businesses, particularly technology and communications equipment suppliers and their parts manufacturers, found themselves with significant unused capacity as one customer after another collapsed causing not only a loss of demand from that customer but also from the state of the art equipment which was being sold in the marketplace as companies were downsized or liquidated. At the same time many of their remaining customers were reducing spending to reduce costs and preserve cash.

All of the above factors result in stock market indexes and the economy behaving in a fashion similar to Newton's Law of motion. Namely, a body in motion tends to remain in motion in the same direction unless impeded by an opposing force. We have observed that when the market rises, except for occasional dips which are viewed as buying opportunities, it is like an upward spiral with stock price increases fueling economic prosperity and individual wealth, which in turn encourages stock market purchases. Similarly when the market declines, except for short rallies it has a depressing effect on the economy which sends stock prices spiraling lower causing a negative wealth effect which further weakens the economy. It helps to explain the current weakness in the stock market and the economy.

Except for specific events which affect the price of one or more securities, stock prices tend to move up and down in tandem influenced by the various technical factors discussed above. With the benefit of hindsight we can observe that these technical factors were the real Y2K problem. Since the investing game results in stock prices exaggerating their lows in falling markets, often the best time to invest is after a precipitous drop in which all of the negative technical factors have come into play.

THE INITIAL GOVERNMENT RESPONSES

Has our Government taken appropriate steps to reverse the direction of the economy? The year 2000 was the first of three bad years for our economy. The dot com bubble burst, computer sales felt the after effect of Y2K upgrading, corporate earnings had peaked, stock prices were declining and unemployment was beginning to rise. The Fed recognized the change in direction of the economy but apparently afraid it would pump air into the balloon waited until 2001 before it effected a series of interest rate reductions in an attempt to offset the adverse business developments and technical market factors. The Fed had waited too long to act.

At the end of the Twentieth Century our government had collected many billions of dollars of income and capital gains taxes as corporate and personal income rose and people realized large profits from securities transactions. This had led to large surpluses which substantially reduced the National Debt. The tax cuts proposed by President Bush shortly after he took office in 2001, were intended, as promised in his election campaign, principally to return a portion of the government surplus to the people to spend as they wished. Our leaders knew or should have known prior to adopting the tax cut that there would shortly be no surplus and that it was highly likely the federal budget would soon be in deficit. When proposing the tax cut, they relied on overly optimistic revenue projections and apparently failed to recognize the impact of the collapse of the dot coms and the falling stock market indexes.

They should have known that federal tax revenues were going to decline. Unemployed people pay less taxes. Instead, they collect unemployment insurance. People with capital losses don't pay capital gains taxes. Instead they are entitled to deduct $3000 per year from their taxable income. Businesses with losses don't pay income taxes. Instead they are entitled to apply the losses against taxable income going back five years and recover prior tax payments and carry the remaining loss forward.

While the proposed tax cut was being debated before Congress, the President's financial advisors alertly took notice of the impending downturn. They were mindful of the fact that his father had not been reelected because the country came out of recession after his failed bid for re-election, and proposed a modification of the tax cuts to stimulate the economy. To get the tax cut approved by Congress and reduce the overall cost, they delayed the effectiveness of certain provisions which favored high income taxpayers and would have been less stimulative.

They thereby converted the tax cut package into an across the board tax cut which helped all taxpayers. Clearly, the $300 per person reduction, which was added to the tax proposal after the economy turned downward, was intended to put a substantial portion of the tax cut into the hands of people who would spend it immediately to stimulate a turnaround before the next Congressional elections. The Fed's interest rate cuts coupled with the stimulative effect of the tax cuts and particularly the $300 per person reduction seemed to stem the recession. However, the technology and communications sectors continued to decline.

THE EFFECT OF SEPTEMBER 11 AND NEGATIVE DISCLOSURES

Arguments as to whether or not a recovery was underway soon became moot. The events of September 11 occurred causing immediate losses aggregating in the hundreds of billions of dollars and choking off any recovery. The Fed followed with further interest rate cuts, bringing the total number of interest rate reductions in 2001 to 11. Such rate cuts were supplemented by increases in military and homeland security spending and the September 11 outlays.

The stock market indexes turned upward after dropping in reaction to September 11. The optimists again thought the recession was brief and over. Consumer spending was again stimulated by the further reduced cost of borrowing. However, capital spending by business remained weak and the technology companies continued to have substantial unused capacity. Furthermore, some of the leading energy trading and communications companies and other widely held entities, which had been among the star performers in the 90s, reported substantial losses. The stock market declined precipitously and the economy stagnated again.

How could companies which were showing large profits and very substantial book values, suddenly report large losses and file for bankruptcy? We learned that prior financial reports of some entities showing strong balance sheets and large revenues and earnings had used very aggressive, questionable or fraudulent accounting practices to inflate the share price, avoid a loan default or qualify executives for high salaries and bonuses. In some instances they used such accounting practices to conceal liabilities or losses, which in most cases resulted from poor management decisions and badly designed or executed business plans.

The frauds perpetrated by executives and questionable or aggressive accounting practices often didn't cause the business problems, they merely concealed them or exacerbated them, causing the company's stock price to remain high or rise further, and enabled it to have higher than deserved credit ratings and to attract more capital. The disclosure of fraudulent practices and the resulting restatement of prior financial statements often set off a chain of events which severely impacted entities which were already attempting to deal with serious financial problems. When such frauds and accounting practices were disclosed, they set off precipitous declines in the value of the stock and led to lower credit ratings which often caused the company involved to have a cash crisis. Lenders, stockholders and employees of such companies suffered sudden and disastrous consequences in the form of defaulted loans, large investment losses and lost jobs.

THE USE OF LEVERAGE AND BUSINESS EXCESSES

The cause of the precipitous earnings declines suffered by many entities lies in more than fraudulent accounting practices which explain only a small number of the cases. It lies in the fact that in the long upward phase of the cycle, many growth companies with aggressive managements, including some of our most prestigious blue chip companies, leveraged their capital by borrowing money to finance their expansion. In the 90's fast growing companies had little difficulty raising funds by selling securities or borrowing billions of dollars with the assistance of their investment bankers, who earned large profits from the relationship.

They made acquisitions, often substantially above current market prices, or large capital investments in high risk ventures worldwide. They optimistically projected cash flows, which reflected expected growth in the economy, revenues from unproven new businesses, or expected savings from a synergistic acquisition. They believed such projected cash flows would enable them to easily meet their debt obligations as they become due. When they achieved the intended results they benefitted from the leverage and their stock prices rose. However, when the economy peaked and began to decline, the anticipated revenues, earnings and cash flows often failed to materialize. Some companies began to default on their high interest bonds which had affectionately been called "junk" bonds in better times.

Using excessive leverage to finance business growth by acquisition or otherwise creates risks similar to individuals buying on margin. Although corporate borrowing takes many forms and leads to the issuance of a wide array of securities, managements generally attempt to manage their debt maturities so that they will be in a position to meet their obligations as they become due. The problem is that almost all long-term loan agreements contain affirmative and negative loan covenants which if certain conditions are not met or are violated accelerate the time of maturity of the debt, effectively converting long term obligations into demand loans. Such loan covenants take many forms which managements have only limited power to negotiate if they wish to obtain the funds. The more aggressive the management, the greater the risk they will take that they will be able to remain in compliance with, or will be able to obtain a waiver when needed, of the onerous loan covenants which they agree to.

A typical loan covenant will require the borrower to increase earnings and revenues annually, maintain ratios of earnings or cash flow to debt service requirements or ratios of aggregate indebtedness to net worth. They generally become more onerous over time since the borrower is expected to meet its optimistic growth projections which justify the granting of the loan. Companies which meet or exceed their projections as is often the case in a growing economy, benefit from the leverage and have little difficulty in remaining in compliance with or obtaining a waiver or modification of their loan covenants which might not be met because of an unexpected development or because the borrower did not anticipate the effects on the balance sheet or income statement of certain events.

A LIQUIDITY CRISIS

If the earnings or revenues of a highly leveraged entity do not grow as expected, which often occurs in a declining economy, in an industry which has excess capacity, or as a result of a catastrophe such as September 11 then the borrower may find itself out of compliance with its loan covenants. Such borrowers face an immediate default and a liquidity crisis. The liquidity crisis is often exacerbated by the payment of excessive compensation to executives which is ignored in periods of expansion and not always reduced soon enough in troubled times. The lender has the right to call the loan and the borrower generally does not have the ability to repay or refinance its indebtedness.

Fortunately for the borrower it is generally to the advantage of its lenders and investment bankers to attempt to minimize their losses by finding a way to restructure the indebtedness or to arrange additional loans to avoid default on the indebtedness. However the borrowers legal and accounting fees are often substantial and the lenders can be expected to require the borrower to pay a penalty and the lender's legal fees and expenses or to sell certain of its assets or divisions as a condition of the extension or restructuring of the loan.

When a borrower is forced to sell even a profitable business, prospective purchasers, aware of the borrowers liquidity crisis, as expected, seek to obtain bargain purchases. Cash becomes the king. Overextended companies often have to sell a recently acquired division for an amount substantially below the purchase price. The problems encountered by highly leveraged debtors in certain industries have left a growing number of overextended borrowers who, sometimes without warning, find themselves out of compliance with their loan covenants. They suddenly find their credit ratings lowered. If they are able to refinance, they generally must do so at higher rates of interest. If they are unable to restructure their debt or to sell off assets other than at distressed prices, they might need bankruptcy protection to attempt to reorganize in order to survive. The price per share of such entities, even if they avoid bankruptcy, often decline by 90% or more.

The longer the downturn lasts, the greater the number of companies which find themselves unable to remain in compliance with their loan covenants or to meet the repayment schedules of their debt. Their lenders often recognizing that they have loans which are under-collateralized, seek ways to work out the indebtedness in order to minimize their own losses.

The value of many pension funds has been decimated by the decline in stock values and interest rate reductions. Pension funds of some of our largest companies are substantially underfunded. They require substantial additional contributions which are negatively impacting current earnings.

During the years 2001 and 2002 we read almost daily about companies facing reduced credit ratings or a liquidity crisis. Substantial companies, even major industries were devastated. The new wave of selling which followed each negative disclosure exacerbated the fear and distrust of investors and set off further margin calls and encouraged increased short selling.

One company after another has collapsed, filed bankruptcy or disappeared. Others are downsizing, reducing purchases of goods and equipment, cutting costs and reorganizing. As they do so their suppliers are cutting back on production, laying off workers and cancelling plans to expand. Companies have been forced to sell or close divisions or sell assets, often at bargain-basement prices to raise funds to pay debts which are maturing. The illness turned out to be a financial plague.

LOSSES, NEGATIVISM AND LOOKING FOR PEOPLE TO BLAME

Ordinary citizens have watched their retirement savings evaporate as the stock market went into a long and steep decline. Investors who thought, often mindlessly, that they had sound investments, have witnessed the value of their portfolios being decimated. Regardless of their reason or lack thereof for buying the stock, they demand an explanation for the drop in price. They have listened almost daily to allegations of questionable or fraudulent financial reporting by some of our largest and best known corporations many of whose executives sold their shares and pocketed tens of millions of dollars shortly before the companies they controlled made negative disclosures. The frequency of the negative disclosures and size of the write-offs have left investors questioning the soundness of almost all SEC filings and reexamining all of their investments.

Investors who have lost a substantial portion of their life savings or retirement funds, look for people to blame and punish. They are suddenly paying attention to the fact that in addition to excessive stock options, companies paid outrageous salaries, bonuses and expenses to or on behalf of senior executives and that some companies found ways to disguise certain payments of bonuses and expenses when issuing their financial reports. Stock options, the magical securities which were designed to give employees the incentive to maximize their effort and share in the success of the entity without cost to the corporation except for upside dilution, have suddenly fallen into disfavor and are blamed for encouraging fraud.

Negativism is currently rampant. Doom and gloom is being spread by widely watched financial programs on television and by newspapers which seem to revel in every disclosure of wrongdoing and arrest of the alleged culprits. Congressmen and federal and state regulators, who failed to act to prevent or limit the excesses and fraudulent conduct, seek political profit by headline grabbing legislation and demands for the punishment of the wrongdoers. Technical analysts create selffulfilling prophecies as they talk about the market testing its lows and nervous investors heed their warning. Many investors are holding securities with substantial losses which they hope to sell as soon as they get even or recover part of their loss. Others will take tax losses regardless of the value of the stock. Some face margin calls on even a minor drop in the value of their portfolio.

Bearish financial analysts and short sellers seek every opportunity to be heard on TV talk shows. They give advice to sell on internet investment sites and message boards often intended to stampede investors into selling to make their predictions a reality. The SEC should be investigating whether stock markets are being manipulated downward by such practices. If they conclude that they are, they should take immediate steps to end them.

The speculative buying excesses which were fueled by fraud, greed and irrational exuberance have turned into liquidation of securities and redemption of mutual funds based on fear and confusion. Investors have gone from gambling with the casino's money to having lost most of their life's savings, and wondering if they should liquidate all their positions to save what they have left. They are questioning whether they should be invested in equities and debt of corporate America which over the years they had been led to believe was the best way to invest one's retirement savings over the long run.

They realize that as a result of the events which they read about daily, a substantial portion of their funds were transferred to thieves, overpaid corporate executives and greedy wall street firms and their executives and employees. Many unsophisticated investors who joined in the festivities by buying near the top, are selling out of fear and panic and the need to salvage what they have left. The same people who talked of dollar cost averaging in rising markets or of investing in growth stocks to finance their retirement or their children's education, postpone investments as stock prices decline. Stocks that looked attractive at $125 or more a few years ago, do not look like good buys at less than 10% of their former highs.

REGULATORY FAILURES AND THE ROLE OF AUDITORS

Investors have lost confidence in the fairness of the presentation and reliability of financial reports filed with the SEC which are the foundation upon which investment decisions are made. They thought these reports were being scrutinized by the SEC and could be relied on. They thought it was a level playing field. What they failed to realize was that there was a lack of adequate regulation of the securities markets and the securities industry by the New York Stock Exchange and NASDAQ and their member firms and by a complacent, underfunded and greatly understaffed SEC. Congressmen were more interested in granting requests of investment bankers who were large campaign contributors than in protecting investors.

The SEC accounting staff did not have sufficient personnel to adequately evaluate even a fraction of the 34 Act filings by reporting companies. Moreover, instead of concentrating on requiring disclosures that were not misleading and could be understood by experts, the SEC, concerned with the inability of ordinary investors to understand disclosure documents, which a high percentage of them didn't read in any event, adopted rules requiring financial documents to be written in "plain English." This meant that precise language to disclose and describe important information, but was understood only by experts, could not be used. Instead of concentrating on the substantive accuracy of the reports or requesting more complete disclosures, the SEC often asked for inconsequential word changes like changing the words "the Company" to "we". Often because of the plain English rule, the only meaningful disclosures were relegated to financial footnotes.

The greatly understaffed SEC was forced to rely on the auditing firms, which had developed a generally well-deserved reputation for care and integrity, to carefully perform their audits to ensure the accuracy and completeness of the financial statements and financial disclosures. In most instances the reliance was well placed. Most financial statements of American entities have been consistently fairly presented and informative to intelligent investors who spend the time to read them carefully.

However, it should be of no surprise that in such a regulatory environment, greedy corporate officers created imaginative business transactions and aggressive accounting techniques to record them bordering on or crossing the line into illegality. Such managements were permitted to do so by their auditors who in most cases merely acquiesced in the wording used by management to describe a highly complex agreement or transaction which often required estimates and assumptions.

What real choice did the auditors have? These were the client's financial statements which were the responsibility of the Company's management. The auditor's function was to determine that the financial statements were fairly presented.

The auditor's report includes a statement that the audit was conducted in accordance with auditing standards generally accepted in the US which require that the auditor plan and perform the audit to obtain reasonable assurance about whether the financial statements are free of material misstatement. The report states that an audit includes examining, on a test basis, evidence supporting the amounts and disclosures in the financial statements and that it includes assessing the accounting principles used and significant estimates made by management, as well as evaluating the overall financial presentation. It also recites the auditor's belief that its audits provide a reasonable basis for its opinion that the consolidated financial statements are presented fairly, in all material respects.

Auditors who prevent clients from exercising reasonable discretion in preparing their financial statements, will with good reason, soon have fewer clients. As might be expected during the late 1990s, the thieves and some of the high risk-takers retained auditors who gave them the most leeway in exercising management's discretion.

AN OVERREACTION BY CONGRESS AND THE PRESS

Rather than recognize the ordinary workings of the business cycle and the broad range of bad individual and business decisions as the principal causes of the economic problems we are facing or the risk that litigation will further damage our weakened economy, our grandstanding Congressmen have selected a few documented fraud cases to blame for our economic woes. Everyone agrees that those executives who committed fraud should be punished, but we have had strong anti-fraud legislation on the books for over 50 years.

We knew that businesses were involved in complex transactions designed to create short-term profits which have been craved by investors in recent years and that it was an impossibility to describe such transactions in plain English. The financial footnotes, and the omissions therefrom, which are now being dissected, disclosed and described with varying specificity the dealings with affiliates, joint ventures and partnerships. We knew that partnerships were being widely used to keep debt off a company's balance sheet and to improve short-term earnings. As long as stock prices went up most investors didn't care if we could understand these dealings.

We must upgrade financial disclosure without discouraging qualified people from accepting positions as corporate executives and directors or taking risks for fear that they will be charged as criminals, or sued civilly for millions of dollars. Management should be able to make decisions which they believe are reasonable when made, but do not work out as they expect and their company incurs losses or fails to meet its projections. This has become an even greater problem as D&O insurance carriers are denying liability based on fraud in the application even with respect to outside directors who were unaware of the alleged fraud. Ironically, the high cost of defending class action litigation has led to further litigation between the insureds and the insurers.

Our goal should be to regulate corporate governance and financial disclosures in a way that assures that management will act in the best interest of stockholders while creating a level playing field for investors. We must not require or even encourage companies to select management which is unimaginative or afraid to take risks which it believes to be in the best long-term interest of the company.

We must not require companies to become so conservative and to always assume the worst case when making financial estimates and assumptions used in preparing their financial reports, that their businesses will be adversely impacted. Management must be permitted to use its own optimism, if reasonable at the time, when making such estimates and assumptions.

It is probable that most of the discredited business schemes, even those which involved large payments to the participating executives, began with a plan intended to benefit the company. Have we forgotten that Yankee ingenuity and risk taking has helped us to develop the greatest economy in the history of mankind? America has shown the world that when you have the freedom to pursue your dreams, poor people can create imaginative new products and business concepts and become rich. Our economy has prospered and the standard of living has improved for almost all of our people who are able and willing to work hard.

Our press, our regulators and Congress are adding to the loss of confidence of Americans in our businesses and our government by attacking one weakened or staggering business after another. Some of the criticism is well-founded, but they seem unaware of the further damage they are inflicting. Many innocent people were partners, stockholders in or worked for and developed a substantial equity in these companies. There is a risk of further stock price declines and job losses. We have a history of providing assistance to important companies facing a liquidity crisis. We should have helped those entities which had been wronged by their executives rather than taking steps which ruined them financially and caused thousands of hard working people who did not partake in any wrongdoing to lose their jobs and their equity. The wrongdoers could have been removed and banned from being associated with management of a publicly owned entity. Doing so would likely have proven beneficial to our overall economy.

THE PROBLEMS OF THE INVESTMENT BANKS

Our investment banking companies have been among the hardest hit by the stock market collapse. They have many serious problems to contend with. Customers of our renowned financial institutions have lost tens of billions of dollars on securities which they underwrote. Important segments of their businesses have shrunk or disappeared. The new issue business which generated billions of dollars of profits has ground to a halt and their loans to and investments in high risk ventures have generated substantial losses and the potential for additional losses. Their own stock prices have declined. Many thousands of their highly paid employees have lost their jobs and others are likely to follow if revenues and profits continue to decline. Their problems have exacerbated the loss of investor confidence and the decline in stock prices. It has made financing of existing businesses more difficult and limited the formation of new ventures. It has negatively impacted out economy and continues to weaken the prospects for a strong recovery.

As a result of the failure of the SEC to enforce the securities laws state attorney generals have stepped to the fore in doing so. They have dusted off and are applying rarely used state fraud laws. Much attention has recently been given by the press, to the investigations by the New York Attorney General into the fraudulent and misleading reports of certain security analysts. They point to the infamous and ridiculously stupid e-mails from analysts, probably written in jest, as proof of fraud. Even personal relationships between those analysts and management are being fine tooth-combed to attempt to link management to wrongdoing.

It is apparent from the settlements made with the New York Attorney General and articles in the press that certain securities analysts at large brokerages attempted to support the share prices of securities which their investment banking divisions were funding, acting as consultant for or partnering with, by issuing highly suspect positive recommendations. Certain of the analysts, whose opinion turned negative about a company they had championed, nevertheless continued to write positive recommendations relating to such companies. Clearly such a practice is wrong and the offenders should be jailed, fined, fired or barred from the securities' industry.

The importance of these tainted recommendations has been blown out of proportion and threatens to cripple or destroy our investment banking industry. We knew that brokerages were recommending stocks for which they we serving as investment bankers. The conflict of interest of the brokerage releasing the report was generally disclosed in a boiler plate statement at the bottom of every report. Such statement also routinely states the obvious, namely that the report speaks as of the day released and the brokerage does not have an obligation to update it. If the investor read the report days after it was released or purchased the shares after the stock had risen, how do we know if the analyst would have recommended the purchase at the later date or at the higher price?

Why should we expect an analyst to risk losing favor with his employer, by writing a negative report about his employer's investment banking client? It was easier to have faith that the company being reviewed would continue to meet its quarterly financial projections as it had in previous quarters with imaginative accounting and the assistance of the firm's investment bankers. If the analyst believed that the slowdown in the economy would be short-lived, he might conclude that a decline in the company's revenues and earnings would soon be reversed or that an across-the-board stock market recovery was imminent. We know that he had an incentive to view the firm's clients positively since writing favorable reports about company clients often led to the receipt of raises and bonuses. Possibly the analysts considered it irrelevant to recite negative news that was already reported in the press or was obvious.

We should take note that most people in the industry paid little credence to those reports. It is questionable as to whether a material number of sophisticated investors relied on them or even paid much attention to them. Why should they have? They knew of the conflict of interest and that the analysts who kept recommending stocks that were declining looked like fools. Investors who receive bad advice can be expected to take their business elsewhere.

THE LITIGATION DISEASE

There has been an outbreak of the litigation disease which is spreading throughout the brokerage community. Although the New York State Attorney General did not bring criminal charges purportedly to limit civil actions, his attacks and attacks by other government representatives and the press against our large banks and investment bankers are further eroding investor confidence and aiding and encouraging civil litigation. The large number of cases may eventually result in claims totaling in the hundreds of billions or even trillions of dollars which will distract management, might lead to excessive damage awards, and will cost tens of billions of dollars to defend, which will further damage such financial institutions.

Class action attorneys, always following the business news like the ambulance chasers of old, race to bring class actions whenever stock prices decline after negative news. When companies restate earnings or fail they pounce on former executives, the investment bankers and anyone else they can think of who has "deep pockets" with which to pay for large claims.

The fear of or commencement of class action lawsuits often causes the shares of companies that make a negative disclosure to decline by an amount which greatly exceeds the amount warranted by the negative disclosure. As a result class actions which in theory are brought to benefit wronged stockholders often cause additional damage to those persons who remain as stockholders after negative disclosures. Many settlements will serve only to enrich lawyers and will lead to meaningless recovery per share for the aggrieved stockholders.

The NYSE suitability rule has long been in place to protect customers of member firms from making inappropriate investments. If the rule is violated a customer can demand an NASD arbitration to recover his losses. It is easy to apply when a customer with a low-risk profile is urged to invest a substantial portion of his assets in a speculative oil drilling or uranium exploration venture.

Many low-risk tolerant investors who were conservatively invested switched their account to a broker whose customers were making large profits investing in technology stocks. There were many investment experts who felt that buying growth stocks, even those with high price-to-earnings ratios, was the best way to earn a return on capital in the long run. With the benefit of hindsight many investors can now argue that their portfolio, which may have consisted exclusively of technology stocks which collapsed, was not suitable for them. However, they were the stocks whose shares had skyrocketed and which large numbers of investors wanted to own.

Most of the investors, sophisticated or not, who chose to switch from conservative to high-risk investments did so because they expected to double their rate of return. They knew or should have known that securities which offer a much higher potential return also involve greater risk. We must not make our brokerages guarantors. People who invest in securities which are at the time of the investment believed to be acceptable risks to make money, must be prepared to suffer losses if their investments go down in value and not up.

Some individuals who lost money now claim they relied on a deceitful or unsuitable recommendation and seek attorneys to try to get their investment back. Much can be said for the doctrine of "caveat emptor". How does one prove that they bought the stock in reliance on the recommendation? Why didn't the investor seek other opinions about the stock? Why didn't the investor follow the developments and sell the stock to limit his loss? Brokerages have already paid penalties which exceed any possible gain they obtained from the tainted recommendations.

Although we must pursue and punish the individual wrongdoers, we must seek to revitalize the investment banking industry if we are going to return our economy to prosperity. We will not be able to do so if we fill our court dockets with cases attempting to recover hundreds of billions or trillions of dollars in damages based on claims of fraudulent, inept or conflicted recommendations made by a few arrogant, corrupt or ignorant financial analysts, which few investors reasonably relied on. We should not forget that many of the same investors, who profited from following recommendations of questionable merit during the market rise, are not being asked to return such profits.

The complexity of the claims virtually assures that our legal system with its mediocre judges and juries incapable of understanding the merits of a complex financial dispute or calculating the damages, often involving billions of dollars, will fail to deliver just verdicts.

What might the same incompetent jury that awarded $28 billion of punitive damages in a tobacco case, award in a case where it is claimed that misled investors lost billions of dollars because of a fraudulent stock recommendation? If the litigation continues without bounds some of our largest financial institutions like the defendants in the asbestos litigations may ultimately need to seek bankruptcy protection.

Tobacco litigation is a prime example of how our court system has lost sight of reality. It is arguable that all tobacco litigation should be dismissed because our Federal and state governments, which raise large sums from cigarette taxes and have extorted tobacco companies into paying large settlements, have not made the sale of tobacco products illegal. The overriding fact in every one of these cases is that everyone has known or should have known for more than 50 years that smoking causes heart and lung diseases and that nicotine is addictive. Most smokers voluntarily take the risk because of the relaxation and enjoyment they receive. They choose to live with rather than to fight the addiction.

Product liability claims have also gotten out of hand. We are using current standards and hindsight to punish companies and even entire industries for producing and selling products which have caused harm, but which were not banned at the time the claim arose. Excessive jury awards of punitive damages and for pain and suffering are punishing current stockholders for decisions made years before by prior management in a much different business environment. It seems that every few years another industry is faced with trillions of dollars of claims.

How many of our important auto companies are we going to seriously damage or force into bankruptcy before we place a limit on the amounts sympathetic juries award to scarred and injured plaintiffs. The real cause of some of the injuries is driver negligence which cannot be demonstrated. We cannot erase the harm which has incurred. Even if the injury might have been preventable, we do not correct the problem by causing financial damage to stockholders and tens of thousands of innocent employees who might lose their jobs or pension benefits as a result of the claims. We permit devastating claims against auto companies for creating hazardous conditions, but do not reward them for developing safety features which save lives and prevent injuries.

On the other hand, class actions should be distinguished from derivative suits which are brought on behalf of the corporation to recover damages for the corporation. Derivative actions against corporate executives are appropriate where it can be proven that the executives fraudulently manipulated earnings to become entitled to receive large bonuses or option grants.

RELIANCE ON ANALYST RECOMMENDATIONS

In this age of rapidly disseminated information the market price of a security generally reflects all available information relating to the issuer. The "random walk" theory of investing is based on this observation. Its advocates believe that only unanticipated future developments are not already reflected in the price of a security. They question whether we can expect an analyst to know something about a security that other analysts do not also know and is not reflected in the price of the stock. This theory became largely discredited because during the 90s analysts were able to consistently recommend stocks which went up. Beginning in the year 2000 analysts who recommended purchases of securities were consistently wrong. It is difficult for followers of the random walk theory to anticipate the effect of market trends but much can be said for the market price of securities reflecting all available information.

A capable analyst may be able to better interpret available information about a company's prospects or have a better understanding of an industry or market conditions. However, it is unusual for an analyst to be able to unearth more than occasionally an exceptional opportunity which others have overlooked. Yet, when an analyst recommends one or two stocks which rise appreciably, investors rush like lemmings to purchase whatever he recommends next. This may temporarily drive the price of such security to an unrealistically high level from which it can be expected to decline over time. We have found in recent years that analysts who recommend the purchase of securities while the market is climbing often disseminate a self-fulfilling prophecy and sale recommendations in a falling market often have the same result.

It has never been a good idea to rely on a brokerage recommendation without having a plan for keeping current on the company involved. Brokerages rarely advise you when to sell because when they do so, particularly in a weak market, the news is disseminated quickly and the stock plummets before most of the brokerage's customers can sell. Criticism of analysts for not putting out downgrades or sell recommendations is unfair. What help is it to investors who have bought a security on an analyst's advice, if the market price of the security declines precipitously after a downgrade or sell recommendation is circulated and before such investors have the opportunity to sell? If an analyst or a broker selects customers to advise in advance, he is accused of playing favorites, which is true, but is inevitable. No investor can reasonably expect to be the customer they call first. There is and should not be any obligation to update an analysts recommendation or to notify recipients of a report, if an analyst changes his opinion with respect to a security.

Now that the market has been battered, brokerages and their analysts have found it fashionable to issue negative recommendations on selected issuers, industries or the market in general. This may help prevent potential purchasers from buying a security at an excessive price, but does little for existing stockholders who find their equities have declined as a result.

We can require brokerages to build "Chinese Walls," but as long as we permit investment banking firms to issue reports of analysts and have brokers who recommend the purchase of securities which the investment banking firm has an interest in or a relationship with, investors will have to remain skeptical of the advice they receive. Furthermore, no matter how flat we make the disclosure playing field, not all management projections or decisions will work out as anticipated. There is no way to avoid the fact that investors must face all of the risks faced by the business they are investing in. If they select companies which outperform the results anticipated by the "Street" they will generally make money. There will be exceptions during periods when the market is in a general state of decline.

CREATING A LEVEL PLAYING FIELD

There are many steps which can be taken to level the playing field and protect stockholders. In recent years we have recognized the importance of having the federal securities laws cover a number of aspects of corporate governance The law changes contained in the Sarbanes-Oxley Act of 2002, which was hastily enacted, are intended to address various problems which affect our corporations and our securities markets. They are designed among other things to upgrade audit committees, improve auditing standards, auditor independence and attorneys' responsibility, enhance financial disclosures, hold additional corporate executives responsible for the accuracy of their company's financial reports and prevent certain practices such as loans to executives which led to abuses. They will improve auditing procedures and limit some of the fraudulent disclosures. However, certain of the requirements of said act are not clear or practical, will result in higher auditing and legal fees and may prove to be counterproductive and should be modified.

For example the no-loan-to-executives rule immediately brought into question whether companies can purchase split dollar insurance or advance the legal fees to enable officers and directors to defend themselves, long standing practices permitted under the laws of most states. The SEC is taking too long to issue regulations to clear up some of the undesired consequences of the wording of the act.

Auditors should be permitted to give guidance in connection with the client's establishing or modifying its internal controls, which the auditor is best situated to give and which are important tools used to improve corporate governance and financial disclosures.

There are many other important problems not dealt with by the Sarbanes-Oxley Act. Fair disclosure requires an examination of a company's financial statements by someone other than an auditor selected by and compensated by management. The SEC accounting staff should be significantly enlarged and should review many additional financial statements including the annual reports of our country's largest 1000 entities.

Companies which determine a substantial portion of their revenues, earnings or expenses based on estimates should be required to disclose the risks which might result from adjustments in such estimates. Where appropriate the SEC might require additional disclosure in a manner that can be understood by sophisticated investors and analysts concerning the methods used in arriving at the estimated amounts.

We have learned from the recent disclosures of outrageous salaries, bonuses and expense reimbursements, that there are insufficient controls relating to the compensation of corporate executives. Said differently the foxes have been in charge of the chicken coops. Delaware has long been the state of choice in which to incorporate because its laws and its courts give the directors and executives almost unfettered control of the corporation. Until recently it was believed this was in the best interest of the stockholders.

COMPENSATION COMMITTEES

The recent disclosures are leading us to a reconsideration as to the need for procedures to make the directors and executives more accountable to the stockholders. We have learned that the requirement of having compensation committees has achieved only limited success. Executive salaries and bonuses aggregating in excess of $25,000,000 per year coupled with stock option grants which could yield another $1,000,000,000 or more, which were granted by compensation committees, were clearly excessive. There is currently no requirement that the members of the compensation committee be independent. In many cases friends of the CEO serve on the compensation committee. Even now when profits have fallen and employees are being laid off or taking pay cuts, many executives are continuing to receive excessive salaries. We must find ways to make compensation committees independent. We might, without impinging on their discretion, give guidance to compensation committees by allowing stockholders to check off a box in the proxy indicating whether they believe that the compensation during the prior year of the company's executive officers was excessive or reasonable.

We relied on the assumption, which we have learned does not always apply, that if management sought to make money for themselves, all stockholders would benefit. While compensating executives based on performance is desirable, we have learned that performance should not be measured over too short a period of time. The events of recent years have demonstrated that stockholders can be hurt if officers can in a legal manner manage earnings by controlling the timing of the receipt of certain revenues and delaying certain expenses. This enables the entity to show an earnings spurt over a period of one or two quarters during which executives might qualify for a large bonus or they can exercise their options and sell the underlying shares.

LIMITING SALES BY INSIDERS

Section 16 of the Exchange Act is based on a presumption that Officers, Directors and beneficial owners of 10% or more of a company's shares have access to inside information when trading their company's shares which might be impossible to prove. While it limits in and out trading by insiders, it does not prevent insiders from cashing out large positions. Since the Sarbanes-Oxley Act does not require the filing of a report of sale until two days after the sale, insiders remain able to unload large positions prior to filing. We might consider requiring insiders to file a notice of intent to sell at least a few days prior to sale or entering into a contract to sell. We might also consider expanding Section 16 to limit the percentage of the Company's shares or of his holdings sold or agreed to be sold by an insider in any quarterly, six month or annual period. This would encourage management to be more concerned with the long-term prospects of the company and would prevent insiders from jumping off a "sinking ship."

REPORTING AND TERMS OF STOCK OPTION GRANTS

Although much attention is being paid to deducting the value of stock option grants as an expense, since the charge against earnings will be a non-cash charge, requiring such a charge will probably be ignored by analysts and investors in the same manner that they ignore restructuring charges. Stock options are a wonderful way, without negatively impacting cash flow, to give incentives to employees, including executives, based on the success of the enterprise. They often provide a source of funding to small cap enterprises.

Improving the reporting of stock option grants would be of great benefit to analysts and investors. At present a company's proxy statement generally discloses option grants during the previous year, but does not disclose non-exercisable grants made after the close of the last fiscal year. Therefore options may be granted a year prior to disclosure. Under present accounting procedures the negative impact of options on fully diluted earnings is often substantial if the price of the stock rises and the number of outstanding options represents a significant percentage of total shares outstanding. Clearly we should require prompt disclosure of large option grants to corporate executives.

Although options may vest over a period of time, the holder is generally permitted to exercise all or any of the vested options during the remainder of the term. We might consider laws which require large options to be exercisable only over a period of years so that executives will be more concerned with the long-term growth of the company. We might also consider tax incentives to encourage option grants which have an increasing exercise price over time to reflect anticipated increases in share price which might result from inflation or the company's reinvestment of earnings.

PROXY RULE CHANGES

One way to ensure that management becomes accountable to and is acting in the best interest of the stockholders is for stockholders, particularly mutual funds, to take a more active role in the process of selecting directors. This has been taking place to a limited extent in recent years. However, we might consider a change in the proxy rules to facilitate the procedure for stockholders to communicate with management and each other in selecting a slate of nominees if they so desired.

We could also provide for reimbursement of their costs of proxy solicitation if a predetermined percentage of shares indicated to management prior to the filing of a company's proxy statement that they wished to put forward an opposition slate.

MORE FINANCIAL PROBLEMS AHEAD

There are more financial clouds overhead. We can expect to continue to hear negative disclosures from major corporations about loan defaults and losses resulting from changes in the valuation of certain assets or investments, accounting restatements, theft and unauthorized and excessive compensation of executives which might drive stock prices even lower. Assumptions will have to be adjusted to reflect experience. Loss reserves will have to be established or increased, often more than once (just as they were with respect to asbestos, tobacco, drug and environmental claims), as current reserves prove to be inadequate to cover litigation claims and operational, investment and bad debt losses. They will be further impacted when determinations with respect to the assets and liabilities of the bankrupt entities are made by the bankruptcy court judges and as civil litigations relating to dealings with such entities are resolved by settlement or court decision. Disputed insurance claims will ultimately be resolved with either the insured or the insurer in many cases realizing losses greater than the reserves which have been established.

The lost income and purchasing power from the huge losses suffered by individuals pension and retirement funds will be felt each year as people retire. Many people who sold securities and purchased expensive homes and cars have seen their remaining portfolios decline appreciably. The negative wealth effect from falling stock prices has been offset in part by the wealth created by the housing boom, but may yet impact auto sales and other consumer spending or the housing boom and thereby impede an economic recovery or lead to a further decline.

Many employees of the failed or troubled companies have lost their jobs. They are finding it difficult to find jobs at or near their prior salary level. Some of them are living by incurring credit card debts. Others are living off the equity in their homes by spending the proceeds received from refinancing their mortgage or by taking out a home equity loan which they set up while still employed and using it to pay off credit card obligations or to support their lifestyles. Others are spending out of capital. Some may soon be unable to meet the carrying costs of their homes. Retired people who used to pay their bills each month are now running up credit card balances. Spending will be constrained as more people exhaust their savings or reach their credit limits.

The credit card companies which extended credit freely, and often without regard to credit worthiness of the cardholder whom they charged what used to be considered usurious interest rates, find themselves facing an increasing number of defaults. The risk is enlarged as cardholders who reach their credit limits on one card, obtain other cards. As more people lose their jobs or spend their capital this number can be expected to continue to rise.

THE HOUSING BOOM

In many cities homes have increased in value at a much greater rate than the cost of replacement. The housing boom has been stimulated by various factors including population growth and limited land in certain desirable areas. However, the most important reason for increased demand is falling interest rates which made mortgage payments more affordable. If interest rates rise from the current lows of recent years, demand for homes and the sales price can be expected to decline as carrying costs increase. A rise in interest rates would also make it impossible to save interest charges by refinancing one's mortgage which has served in recent years as a stimulus to consumer spending.

The rapid rise in home values, the numerous refinancing of homes, many of which increased the amount of the mortgage and reduced the homeowner's remaining equity and the granting of home equity loans, have left banks more vulnerable to a decline in home values. Unless we see an upturn in the economy which creates new high paying jobs we may see defaults by unemployed individuals leading to foreclosures which could set off a precipitous decline in home values. To the extent that banks have packaged and resold these mortgages as derivatives, the risk of loss after default has been passed on to the holder of the derivative security.

If and when the banks attempt to reduce the risk by lending a smaller percentage of the home equity, home purchases will become out of reach of some potential buyers. If the prices of homes stagnate or decline, borrowing for home improvements and to finance the owners living expenses will be curtailed. The risk of declining home prices may also be expected to increase as states, counties and cities, facing large declines in income tax revenues and resulting deficits, raise real estate taxes to generate needed revenues. Such tax increases will make homes less attractive as investments and less affordable.

The risk that there is a bubble in the housing market and of a possible collapse of the price of homes makes it imperative that we take steps now to limit the number of defaults by stimulating our economy so that it turns upward and grows at an acceptable rate.

RISK OF DEFLATION OR COLLAPSE

Instead of companies attempting to increase their short-term profits by growing their revenues, they are attempting to do so by laying off employees and downsizing, which negatively impacts GDP and threatens to set off a deflationary spiral. Laying off employees as a way to increase profits does not speak well of the ethical considerations of management in dealing with employees. The decline in union membership over the last 30 years, though on the whole beneficial to our economy, did have the effect of weakening job security which slowed past declines in GDP.

Our Government's unemployment statistics are unreliable. Millions of laid off workers are collecting unemployment insurance or have found ways to collect disability or workmen's compensation payments and have switched family roles with their spouses who are now working, often at lower pay, to support the family. Many people have given up looking for work. Because of the Government's absurd definition of unemployment they are not counted in the ranks of the unemployed. The number of long-term unemployed continues to grow as technology, aircraft and investment banking companies, among others, continue to lay off employees. Ironically technology improvements which increase worker productivity are reducing manpower needs and contributing to unemployment.

Most states and cities are required by law to balance their annual budgets. States and cities facing declining tax revenues and increasing expenses are looking for ways to control spending or increase taxes. Even if the stock markets stage a recovery many investors have substantial capital loss carry-forwards or unrealized losses and will not have to pay capital gains taxes. Some states which tax estates to the extent of the Federal Estate Tax credit are receiving declining revenues as a result of the phase-in of changes in the Federal Estate Tax eliminating the state estate tax credit which were adopted when state budgets were showing surpluses despite the known negative impact on state estate tax revenues. States and cities faced with the need to increase their efforts to prevent future terrorist acts are unable to do so because of a lack of funds. They are being forced to reduce payrolls and services. There is little prospect that they will obtain sufficient Federal assistance to prevent further layoffs or provide adequate security against further acts of terrorism.

Investors' worst fears may prove justified. The interest rate cuts by the Fed in 2001, and the stimulative tax cuts appeared to stem the initial downturn. But, in light of the disclosures during 2002, it seems clear that the stimulus was woefully inadequate and that the upturn which some economists believed was developing was not sustainable. We have learned that the stock market excesses of the 90s greatly exceeded those of the 20s.

The market averages' inability to mount a sustained recovery from multi-year lows are telling us that we do not yet know the cumulative effect of the following on our economy; (i) the losses resulting from the events of September 11, (ii) poor management decisions of our corporate executives, (iii) the funding of ill conceived and poorly managed businesses by our banks and investment bankers, (iv) the fraudulent and misleading disclosures not prevented by auditors and regulators, (v) the greed of investors who bid up stock prices to unsupportable levels and recklessly purchased new issues, (vi) the exacerbating effects of falling stock prices resulting from margin liquidations, short selling, stop loss orders, program selling, chart theories, mutual fund redemptions, and investor fears, (vii) the consequences of excessive debt of businesses and individuals (viii) the compensation abuses of corporate executives, (ix) the need of some people to protect their remaining funds, (x) the risk that our economy will suffer if oil prices or interest rates rise, (xi) the cumulative effect of corporate downsizing and reducing the number of employees and (xii) the risk of a material decline in the prices of homes.

Whatever steps we take to improve our economic system by changing our laws which are the rules of the games of business and investment, they will be felt over a period of time but are not going to have an immediate impact on our economy. The events of September 11 and the collapse of a large number of internet and communications companies (many of which had collapsed or experienced serious financial problems before September 11) resulted in investment losses by individuals and businesses aggregating trillions of dollars and rendered other important companies including many banks (which as usual got caught up in the euphoria of good times and made highly risky investments and loans secured by overvalued assets) and insurance companies less able to withstand further setbacks.

Reports that the leading market indicators indicate that our economy is expanding are again likely prove to be short-lived. Businesses have excess capacity, are not purchasing capital items and realize that they can get by without the latest technology. The numerous interest rate cuts have not significantly stimulated business investment and the proposed tax cuts are not likely to do so. Businesses will not purchase new and improved technology until demand increases substantially or they determine that it is cost effective or that it is required to remain competitive. As companies continue to downsize there will be additional layoffs.

The falling stock market, reduced investment income, loss of jobs, loss of confidence in our financial markets and institutions and in our economy and rising oil and gas prices and state and local taxes, make it more likely that our debt-laden consumers will reduce purchases rather than increase them. This might result in a downturn in all consumer dependent industries including housing, home construction, home improvement, appliances, clothing and automobile manufacturing.

Our economy faces the risk of continued stagnation, double dip recession, deflation or even collapse. The risk is multiplied by the likelihood that future terrorist acts, especially one which involves a weapon of mass destruction, will further damage our economy.

It is a world economy. It is said that if the U.S. catches a cold, the world gets pneumonia. Our weakness has caused a worldwide downturn and some of the weaker nations are facing steep downturns and have seen their currencies collapse. Some South American economies are in ruin. Others may follow if the World Bank does not take preventative action. Many European and Asian economies are in a slump and are not being adequately stimulated. The problems of our trading partners negatively impact our exports. Our international companies are being hurt by anti-American sentiment worldwide. In times like these, countries turn to import duties or export supports to assist their inefficient producers in retaining market share. Such actions hurt all of the players because they reverse the benefits of free trade.

The Japanese have learned that recession and deflation are like a cancer. Prevention is the preferred approach and the longer we wait to deal with the symptoms the more serious the problem becomes. In the game of macroeconomics, inflation has long been feared, but until recently we have overlooked the fact that deflation causes vastly more harm than inflation.

Our Government recognized during 2001 that the rise and fall of the economy also follows the principals of Newton's laws of motion. While the substantial stimulus that was provided in the form of interest rate reductions and tax cuts might have been expected to be adequate to return our economy to prosperity during normal conditions, the actual events of the past 18 months were far from normal. They were much more negative then were anticipated.

LACK OF IMPETUS FOR SUBSTANTIAL GROWTH

Our survival as a prosperous nation is more vulnerable than at any time since the 1930's. Even if we avoid a double dip recession, we currently have no impetus for substantial growth. Our internet and telecommunication industries will consolidate and begin to grow again, but we can not look to them to lead us back to prosperity.

Too many losses have been suffered by too many people, for too many reasons. Investors, with good cause, have lost confidence in many of our leading corporations, our Government regulators and legislators, our brokerages and investment bankers and in the integrity of financial reporting.

Investors do not know whom to trust. As a result many investors will remain on the sidelines until after they see a strong upturn in the economy. It is not likely that investors burned badly during the three year decline will at least for the next few years put most of their investment funds in common stocks. It is extremely unlikely that we will ever again see the high price earnings ratios which were attained by the Dow and NASDAQ.

Questions are raised as to whether the current price earnings ratios remain excessive, even at currently reduced levels. We face reduced and uncertain earnings expectations, risks of terrorism and the fact that sales of autos and homes, two areas which usually lead a recovery, have remained at high levels and may not grow substantially, if at all. Despite these concerns the relatively high price earnings ratios of companies in the major market indexes reflect an expectation that our economy will turn upward and earnings will grow. Many prognosticators are citing this fact as a precursor of a further stock market decline. However, even if they are wrong and the stock markets make a partial recovery, it is unlikely to stimulate spending by either business or individuals.

The new issue market will hopefully revive in the near future to provide risk capital to the next generation of entrepreneurs. However, it is highly unlikely that investors will ever again develop such an insatiable investor appetite for high risk ventures. A much greater number of investors have been involved this time and the losses are much larger than ever before incurred. Investors will be skeptical of even carefully selected issues which they would have rushed to buy a few years ago. Underwriters will have to be more diligent in selecting attractive issuers which will be difficult unless the economy turns upward. Their customers will live by the adage: Fool me once shame on you. Fool me twice shame on me.

The upside potential of offerings will be limited because investors with tax loss carry-forwards are less likely to observe the no-resale rule and as noted above if the issues do not go up appreciably there is no compelling reason to buy them except for their reasonable profit potential. Furthermore, high risk taking investors who have been burned by margin liquidations are not likely to fearlessly leverage their portfolios to maximize purchasing power. Seventy years passed before the irrational exuberance of the 1920s was rekindled in the 1990s.

OUR CURRENT STRENGTHS AND WEAKNESSES

What should our government do now to enable our economy to attain an annual growth rate of 5% or more and return us to a period of prosperity? First we must assess the economy's current strengths and weaknesses.

We might start by noting that stock market losses exceeding $7 trillion and all of the negative business developments which have exacerbated the cyclical business downturn have not caused a severe downturn affecting all industries or a depression. A large percentage of the paper wealth created during the excessive rise in stock prices merely made investors feel richer for a period of time. It enabled them to contemplate a more comfortable retirement. If all the facts had been known, the market would not have risen as excessively and they would not have had as much paper wealth. Fortunately the backbone of spending by our retired workers is protected by Social Security which is not subject to the vagaries of investing in securities. Some of them also have fixed private pensions to rely upon.

As noted above, many individuals benefitted from the advances in technology, the proliferation of the Internet and the dot coms and even from the excesses in the securities markets. While funds were still pouring into equity investments many individuals who had accumulated great wealth on paper determined for any number of reasons to realize profits and turn a substantial portion of their securities into cash. In some cases they did so by exercising stock options and selling the underlying shares in open market transactions. Where required they made SEC filings. They were realizing the American dream. During the 90s and in the years 2000 and 2001 funds which were being saved were transferred from investment, savings and retirement accounts to (i) the hands of individuals in exchange for securities of the companies they had founded and worked for (ii) companies in exchange for newly issued securities (iii) investors selling securities for any number of reasons (iv) investment bankers for commissions, discounts and fees a substantial portion of which was paid to their employees and (v) the US Government and state governments in payment of income and capital gains taxes.

Many of the individuals who benefitted from the growth and prosperity used the money received to invest in other ventures, some of which proved unprofitable, but some of it was spent to acquire expensive homes, cars, and other luxury items and to support their lifestyles. This set off a housing boom and contributed to a strong auto market.

Our economy has a solid core of businesses which benefitted from and are continuing to benefit from the advances in technology, the growth of the Internet and the financing of the new businesses which have survived. The monies invested in even the failed IPOs added to our economic prosperity as it was spent in the ordinary course of their businesses. As a result of the multiplier effect from the recipients spending the funds, the GNP was increased by at least two to three times the amount spent by the IPOs. More than 15 million new jobs were created. All areas of the economy benefitted indirectly from the spending of the IPOs. Many new and beneficial products were developed which greatly improved productivity in all industries. A substantial portion of the funds were spent buying products and services from major Internet companies which accumulated very large cash reserves enabling them to weather the dot com and Internet storm.

It is the nature of capitalism that growth leads to excesses and overcapacity in some industries, which lead to less than anticipated sales and profits for some companies and eventually results as described above in a shakeout of the weakest and most overextended players. In most recessions the economy consolidates and forms a base from which the next growth period can develop when the downward spiral has ended.

We learned in the 1930s that once the stock market collapses and the economy is seriously weakened, our economy requires a very substantial stimulus to end the downturn and generate the growth which can result in an upward spiral. When playing the game of macroeconomics our government must ask what type of governmental stimulus is needed to stop a downward spiral and propel the economy upward. Most of our recent recessions were caused by a decline in consumer demand and were ended by stimulating such demand. Our government attempted to end the recession which began in 2001 by lowering interest rates and taxes to stimulate demand. Although it helped to support consumer spending, it did little if anything to increase capital spending by businesses which were saddled with overcapacity.

The recession which began in 2001 was atypical. It seriously affected certain high technology industries including the dot coms, computer hardware and software, the Internet and telecommunications industries as well as air transportation and aircraft manufacturing. Revenues of companies in industries which had ben-efitted from the wild and unsustainable growth in the 90s but had developed overcapacity or were impacted by September 11, and the suppliers of those com-panies, declined precipitously.

It is rarely the growth companies of the previous expansion which developed excess capacity which lead the next upturn. It is likely that we will need to find another industry to take the lead if we are going to have a substantial upturn in our economy.

Other industries which relied on consumer spending continued to experience growth during the downturn. Auto sales and sales of consumer durables and home improvement products which generally decline in a recession, and often lead the upturn, increased as interest rates declined, home mortgages were refi-nanced and as assets which were being earmarked for retirement and were being saved and not spent, were transferred to people who were prepared to make sub-stantial current expenditures. In addition some individuals, including some who had lost a substantial portion of their savings, decided that real estate was a better investment than securities.

THE GOVERNMENT'S NEXT MOVES IN THE GAME OF MACROECONOMICS

Has our leadership properly assessed and taken appropriate steps to offset the effects which the negative business developments, the stock market declines, the events of September 11, the uncertainty of the effects of a war overseas and the threat of further acts of terrorism, are having on our economy? As difficult as it may be for our government to play the game of macroeconomics under ordinary conditions, the game has become much more complicated as a result of certain governmental practices which have become more prevalent during the past ten years including the extensive use by the executive and legislative branches of our government of unreliable and misleading projections of government revenues and expenditures, the failure of our government to adopt tax and spending prac-tices which are in the best interest of our country rather than of special interest groups and the failure of our government to prevent unfair or illegal business practices and to regulate the securities markets.

The stock market's inability to sustain any rally from the lows, particularly in the bellwether technology issues whose share prices have been battered, is signal-ing a concern that the economy has rough sledding ahead. This is not just another minor recession which can be reversed by a tweaking of our economy. The damage to business and to personal savings has been unparalleled in our history.

We must not be misled by the fact that certain industries have been virtually unscathed by the recession. There is a serious risk that if we do not strengthen the industries which have been negatively impacted, their downsizing and loan defaults and all of the other after shocks of the excesses of the 1990s, the full extent of which has not been adequately reserved or written off, will begin to impact other industries. Recent stock market declines in housing and home improvement companies, as well as in auto and retail stocks, are telling us that this risk is real.

In 2002 the Fed had stepped to the sidelines to observe the developments. It did not act despite the string of negative disclosures which ravaged the stock market. Although it again waited too long before further reducing interest rates, it finally did so in November.

The Fed was obviously concerned that despite increased government spending to support the war in Afghanistan and for cleanup and other losses resulting from the events of September 11 and for homeland security, unemployment was rising and a double dip recession might be developing. Construction of replacement structures at Ground Zero which is important to the revitalization of the New York City economy was (and is still being) delayed while we develop and debate the merits of plans for a memorial and structures to be constructed in the place of the Twin Towers.

We do not know how much benefit we will get from the November 2002 interest rate reductions because home mortgage rates are already the lowest they have been in many years and car loan rates have been at zero for some time.

Although the prior interest rate reductions seem to have prevented a decline in consumer spending, the latest rate cut may not achieve the same result. Lower interest rates are materially reducing the income of our retired people living off the interest they receive from their bonds and CDs. The lower interest rates and the extended period over which they have been reduced leads to a greater percentage of higher interest bonds and CDs maturing or being called. Holders of such investments are finding themselves unable to reinvest the proceeds except at substantially reduced interest rates. Many of such investors have had to reduce their spending or spend out of principal with dire long term consequences as income further declines. Although many retirees have tried to maintain their lifestyles, the longer interest rates remain at current levels or if they decline further, the more of them will face the need to reduce spending.

It is clear that President Bush would like to encourage a rise in the stock markets. However, he seems to have learned that he should not be commenting on stock prices. An elimination of the tax on dividends might help, but probably not significantly. The way to convince Americans that the stock market is the best place for them to invest their retirement funds is to take steps to return our economy to prosperity. Only when companies begin to report or project substantial revenue and earnings growth, will the stock market make a sustainable recovery. The shell shocked public's scepticism and mistrust of corporate financial statements will continue until the stock market recovery is well underway.

Both political parties have indicated an awareness of the need to further stimulate the economy. They both propose that we do so by means of a tax cut. Of course, the Democrats want to repeal the provisions passed two years ago which become effective in future years and substitute a tax cut which will favor lower income people. President Bush should recognize that even if he could justify the tax cuts when adopted in 2001 as a plan to return surplus to the taxpayers who were the prime contributors to that surplus, we now need a tax cut which will provide immediate stimulus to consumer and business spending to prevent the housing, auto and other industries dependent on consumer spending from turning downward and broadening the downturn. He should therefore steal the Democrats' thunder and propose a repeal or delay of the legislated tax cut and substitute a tax cut that will help lower and middle income individuals who will spend it. The effectiveness of the previously enacted tax reductions can be delayed until a more prosperous time when the Federal budget has returned to surplus.

Reducing or eliminating a tax on dividends at the current time would be a terrible mistake. It would substantially increase the deficit, would not likely impact investment, and would benefit the highest income taxpayers who will not spend a high percentage of the tax savings. Cash which might be used to pay dividends might be better used to pay down debt or finance expansion. Securities paying dividends compete with tax exempt bonds which will cause the rates paid by state and local governments to rise. Viewed from the point of fairness, why should corporate dividends be treated differently than interest received on savings which represent after tax earnings?

This is not the time to be making a substantial change in the tax code which will materially reduce future government tax revenues. There are many things wrong with our Federal Income Tax laws of which a tax on dividends is not the most serious. If we were going to make a substantial change we would be better served if we eliminated the outrageous marriage penalty which cheats the middle class out of hundreds of billions of dollars and changed the unfair alternative minimum tax to exclude those persons who have or will become inadvertently become subject to it.

The years of prosperity gave our economy the strength to weather the immediate loss of hundreds of billions of dollars from the events of September 11. Until we take steps to strengthen our economy, our weakened economy will have a much more difficult time in dealing with an event of a similar magnitude. The fear engendered by even a relatively small terrorist attack may seriously impact our economy. Despite the seriousness of the risk that our economy might collapse neither party seems to sense the urgency of stimulating our economy.

Are new tax cuts currently being debated the best course of action for our government to take now in playing the game of macroeconomics? While an across the board tax cut can be expected to stimulate consumer spending and prevent a downturn, it is unlikely to significantly increase capital spending by business which is needed to ignite a recovery in high technology companies. Providing additional investment tax credits to encourage businesses to develop contingency plans and purchase equipment to enable them to continue operations following a terrorist attack would be more likely to encourage capital expenditures.

OUR ECONOMY WILL REQUIRE A MUCH MORE SUBSTANTIAL STIMULUS IN THE FORM OF GOVERNMENT SPENDING TO CREATE NEW JOBS AND GENERATE A DESIRABLE RATE OF GROWTH IN THE TECHNOLOGY SECTOR AND IN THE ECONOMY AS A WHOLE. The increased government spending could come in the form of domestic spending for education, healthcare and other important programs or to repair and replace our aging infrastructure. Such spending would lead to increases in consumer spending and employment but is not likely to significantly impact our ailing industries. Spending on homeland security is not only a more immediate need, but it is more likely to accomplish that task.

THE STIMULUS FROM MILITARY AND HOMELAND SECURITY SPENDING

The current wars at home and abroad are beginning to have a material impact on government spending. Governments generally have only limited control over cost incurred in fighting a war since winning the war is an overriding objective. In past wars we increased military spending principally to support military operations overseas. In the current war we must also spend not only to pursue terrorists throughout the world and to make preventive strikes against nations that threaten our freedom and personal safety, but also to enable us to succeed in carrying out the immense task of defending our homeland.

THE AMOUNT WE MUST SPEND TO WIN THE GAME OF WAR, INCLUDING THE COST OF STRENGTHENING OUR MILITARY, ISSUING AND ACHIEVING MAXIMUM BENEFIT FROM THE US ID AND SEALING OUR BORDERS AS PROPOSED ABOVE, IS GOING TO BE VERY SUBSTANTIAL, FAR IN EXCESS OF THE AMOUNT SPENT ON ANY PRIOR WAR EFFORT. IT IS GOING TO REQUIRE AGGRE-GATE SPENDING OF TRILLIONS OF DOLLARS OVER THE NEXT TEN YEARS. OUR CONGRESS, FEARING DEFICITS, HAS NOT PRO-VIDED SUFFICIENT FUNDING TO DATE. INCREASING THE DEFI-CIT BY SUBSTANTIALLY REDUCING GOVERNMENT TAX REVENUES IN FUTURE YEARS WITHOUT GENERATING A SUB-STANTIAL STIMULUS TO OUR ECONOMY WILL MAKE IT MORE LIKELY THAT CONGRESS, WHICH SEEMS TO HAVE FORGOTTEN AL QAEDA, WILL FAIL TO PROVIDE THE REQUIRED FUNDING EVEN THOUGH SUCH FAILURE WILL JEOPARDIZE THE SURVIVAL OF OUR WAY OF LIFE.

Despite the prospective long term stimulus which will result from the war effort, we are told repeatedly that a war in Iraq will negatively impact the GDP. It is true that as reservists are called up there will be an immediate reduction in pro-duction and spending by such reservists and their families. The price of oil may soar or the supply disrupted further disrupting our economy. On the other hand, some of the jobs vacated may have disappeared as a result of downsizing in any event or another person currently unemployed may be hired to fill the vacancy. The required military expenditures to support the war efforts and enhance our preparedness so that we can fight on multiple fronts if necessary will more than compensate for the temporary decline in spending.

Stimulative tax cuts, a war with Iraq and increases in government spending will swell the short term deficits which we are incurring as a result of the down-turn. We need not fear such deficits. We know from past history that we will be able to bear the resultant debt burden if we see a light at the end of the tunnel. Hopefully, the Fed will take appropriate action to limit any rise in interest rates which might result from increased Government borrowing.

It is clear that if we proceed with an all out effort to improve our homeland defense, the increased spending outlined above will create attractive new business and employment opportunities in the high tech industries. The companies involved in providing services and equipment for the homeland security effort will form the new dynamic growth industry our economy currently needs. It will generate increases in revenues and earnings, improve liquidity and induce hiring, spending on research and development and capital expenditures not only of the companies which will be directly involved in the manufacture of equipment and software for and provide services to the homeland security industry, but also for the high tech businesses which will be their suppliers. The development of the HSN will immediately stimulate the telecommunications industry.

HOMELAND SECURITY SPENDING WILL LEAD TO A SUBSTANTIAL GROWTH ACROSS THE BOARD IN OUR ECONOMY, WHICH WILL GENERATE A RECOVERY IN THE STOCK MARKET. IT WILL IMPROVE THE LIQUIDITY OF OUR BANKS AND OUR BUSINESSES AND REACTIVATE THE CAPITAL MARKETS. IT WILL GENERATE THE TAX REVENUES TO PAY FOR OUR DEFENSIVE EFFORT. BY STIMULATING THE ECONOMY, THE FEDERAL AND STATE DEFICITS THAT ARE BEGINNING TO MUSHROOM AS A RESULT OF THE COLLAPSE OF THE STOCK MARKET, THE DOWNTURN IN THE ECONOMY, THE IMPACT OF THE SEPTEMBER 11 ATTACK AND INCREASING HOMELAND SECURITY EXPENDITURES, WILL TURN OVER A FEW YEARS TO SURPLUSES AS WAS THE CASE IN THE 90S.

By strengthening the economy and returning it to a condition of sustainable growth, we will be more capable of withstanding the effects of further acts of terrorism in the event that we are unable to prevent them. The converse is also true. If we do not increase defense expenditures or otherwise materially increase government spending, the economy, as a result of the confluence of negative events coupled with technical market factors, will continue to stagnate or decline leaving us more vulnerable to collapse from debt defaults, declining consumer spending, a decline in the housing market or as a result of further acts of terrorism.

The homeland security industry will help us to overcome our past failures by becoming the engine that replaces the dot coms and the telecommunication companies in driving the sustained non-inflationary growth of our economy for many years. The irony is that our reaction to the attempts by Al Qaeda to destroy our economy may provide the impetus needed to avoid a deep recession or a depression and return our economy to prosperity.

Playing the game of macroeconomics will be further complicated because spending to finance a war effort generally stimulates growth and prosperity, but under some conditions may cause shortages of labor, raw materials and manufacturing capacity leading to business disruptions and inflationary pressures. We must also be prepared to react to the effects of any future terrorist acts. Intense competition worldwide, and increased productivity generated by technology advances, helped to restrain price increases even during the excesses of the 90s. Inflation should initially be limited by our excess capacity, further productivity gains and potential additions to the work force.

Planning for and Reacting to Terrorist Acts

We must anticipate and take steps to insulate our businesses from the consequences of future terrorist acts which may disrupt production or demand. In recent wars we were able to continue our personal and business activities without inconvenience or interruption. We were able to bear the increased military costs without having to seriously consider personal sacrifices of the type we endured during World War II when we had to ration our resources, work day and night and modify our production to support our war effort. It is therefore not surprising that except for limiting travel (which is partly the result of business cost cutting) we are living our lives as before and generally ignoring the fact that we are at war. We must prepare our people to join the defense effort and sustain personal economic sacrifices if required to do so.

On the other hand we cannot permit terrorism to unnecessarily disrupt our economy. It is difficult to judge the extent to which the sluggishness in the airline industry or the business in New York City is the result of the after effects of September 11 or of the stock market collapse. We should be educating our population about the importance to our economy, in the event of future terrorist attacks, of defying the terrorists and living our lives as close to normal as possible except to the extent required by the defense effort. A strong homeland security network, supported by a US ID card, is instrumental to support such effort.

Airline Regulation

In order to prevent the collapse of our airline industry we should consider the need we may have now or at a future time to regulate the industry or to grant subsidies to the airlines that serve the least traveled routes. The important steps we have taken to make air travel safer are not likely to return air travel to prior levels or ensure that future events might not further reduce the number of passengers.

PROVIDING TERRORISM REINSURANCE

The risk of loss from acts of terror is having a material impact on the insurance industry. As we are learning from the World Trade Center litigation, determining whether an act of terrorism is one event or two events is going to have a very material impact on the recovery. In the future, acts of terrorism may occur seconds or minutes apart or over periods of days or weeks and the aggregate losses may mount. If the same property is attacked twice or multiple times the owner is concerned with the total loss and should not be relegated to litigating an interpretation of the deductible or the definition of an event.

Instead of assuming without charge a portion of the risk of damage and relying on the insurance industry to try to estimate the potential losses which may result from future terrorist acts and find ways to limit their exposure, our government should support the issuance of adequate terrorist coverage by offering for an appropriate fee the highest level of reinsurance. Such reinsurance might cover 90% of losses incurred in excess of a selected percentage such as 20% or 25% of the amount of the coverage on each risk and in the aggregate for all losses incurred anywhere in the US above a predetermined level, from terrorist acts over a period of time, such as one year. We might consider offering reinsurance for terrorist coverage to protect a mortgage lender for the full term of a mortgage.

In addition to property and casualty coverage, the offering of governmental reinsurance should apply to a variety of other types of coverage, including life and health insurance in the event of large numbers of deaths and injuries and business or rent interruption insurance, resulting from acts of terror.

In this way our Government will receive a substantial payment to help finance its costs of performing its function of protecting our citizens and their property. If it can prevent acts of terror it will earn a substantial profit from providing the reinsurance. It will increase the insurance cost to the insured, but will assure them that coverage will be available on a continuous basis.

CONCLUSION

In conclusion, the problems of dealing with homeland security and revving up our economic engine are intertwined and the suggestions above attempt to describe the magnitude of and present an approach for dealing with both problems. The effort will require enormous governmental expenditures and will have to be reassessed on an ongoing basis as we continue to play the games of war and macroeconomics.

If the defensive effort causes inflation or creates a long term debt burden for future generations, which is highly unlikely, so be it. Our children and grandchildren will be the main beneficiaries of our making America safe from terrorism and the revitalization of our economy. Anyhow, the debt burden and risk of inflation is likely to be as great if we do not take further action to stimulate the economy. Today the threat of deflation far outweighs the risk of inflation. To the extent that we do stimulate our economy as proposed above, and over a period of time it causes our economy to grow too fast, which at present is only wishful thinking, we might consider other steps such as an increase in interest rates or a tax increase to slow the excessive growth.

If we can defend our homeland and prevent further harm to our economy as a result of the numerous poor investment and business decisions which were made in the late 1990s and the frauds which are still being uncovered, American capitalism will survive and prosper and we will someday look back and realize that the economic events of the 1990s taken as a whole contributed to the betterment of our lives and the long term growth of our economy.

Does that mean that this is the time to buy common stocks? It is impossible to judge the exact point when the bottom of a downturn has been reached, but if our Government takes appropriate actions, informed investors who begin to accumulate shares of quality securities which they believe are undervalued, can expect to earn a favorable rate of return on their capital invested over the long run.

0-595-27142-1

CPSIA information can be obtained
at www.ICGtesting.com
Printed in the USA
BVOW08s2052140617

486954BV00001B/25/P